Sorry I Was Late to My Own Life

Productivity for People Who've Already Wasted Half the Day

I.L. Hartley

Published by
Pen Tillman
Tillman Forsyth Publishing House

tillmanforsythpublishings@gmail.com

v.1.0.08

1

This page is intentionally left blank.

Table of Contents

Author's Note:

First of all, congratulations. If you are reading this, it means you actually opened the book. You didn't just buy it and let it sit on your nightstand as a literary paperweight while you watched three hours of "How to be Productive" videos on YouTube. That's a win. Write it down. We're counting it.

Here is the deal: I am not a productivity guru. I do not wake up at 4:00 AM to plunge into an ice bath, nor do I have a color-coded spreadsheet for my spice rack. In fact, I wrote large portions of this book while wearing mismatched socks and ignoring a mounting pile of laundry that has since achieved sentience. I am not even an expert.

I am a recovering chronic starter. I have wasted more Tuesday afternoons than I care to admit, usually by getting emotionally invested in the Wikipedia page for 17th-century tulip bubbles or deciding that 2:00 PM is the perfect time to reorganize my digital photos from 2014.

This book is a **No-Judgment Zone**.

The stories you'll read in here are true-ish (names have been changed to protect the equally disorganized). The advice, however, is very real. These are the "Tiny Rebellions" I had to invent just to get my own life back on track when the standard, high-performance advice felt like it was written for a different species.

We aren't aiming for perfect in these pages. We're aiming for slightly better than yesterday. That's why I am writing this book. Because if you are reading it, it means not only have I started it, but I have finally finished it (yay to me!).

So, if you've already wasted half the day, don't worry about it. The second half is still up for grabs. Let's stop apologizing for being late to the party and actually start enjoying the music. Stay messy, but stay moving. Now, given this entire book is about productivity (or lack thereof), let's see if you can finish this thing…

— I.L. Hartley

P.S. Please note: I write this book as less of a "how-to" guide and more of a conversation.

Introduction: Welcome to the Late Party

If you are reading this in the middle of a Tuesday afternoon while surrounded by half-empty coffee mugs and a to-do list that looks more like a cry for help than a plan of action—welcome. You're among friends.

I'm going to take a wild guess: you woke up this morning with the best of intentions. You were going to be a productivity powerhouse. You were going to crush your inbox, meal prep a kale salad, and finally figure out what that weird rattling noise in your car is.

Then, something happened. Or rather, nothing happened. You checked one email, which led to a LinkedIn rabbit hole, which led to wondering if your high school chemistry teacher is still alive, which led to a forty-minute deep dive into the history of artisanal sourdough starters. Suddenly, it's 2:00 PM. The sun is starting its slow descent, and you are sitting there with a heavy, cold knot in your stomach that says: Well, the day is basically over. I'll just start for real on Monday.

The "Wasted Day" Myth: We've all been sold a lie. The lie is that productivity is a sunrise-to-sunset performance. We're told that if you didn't win the morning, you've already lost the war. We treat our days like a fine China plate—the moment there's one tiny crack in the schedule, we figure we might as well smash the whole thing on the floor and try again with a fresh plate tomorrow.

I am here to tell you to stop smashing the plates.

This book isn't for the people who have it all figured out. It's not for the CEOs who run marathons before breakfast or the influencers whose desks are perpetually cleared of everything except a single succulent and an expensive candle.

This book is for the rest of us. The ones who feel like we're constantly running ten minutes behind our own potential.

Why This Book is Different: Most productivity books are written by people who naturally love systems. They find joy in filing. They get a dopamine hit from a well-organized closet.

I am not one of those people. I am a person who once spent three hours researching "best ergonomic office chairs" as a way to avoid sitting in my current chair and actually working. I know every trick the human brain uses to avoid doing the Hard Thing.

In the chapters that follow, we aren't going to talk about optimization or synergy. We're going to talk about the recovery. We're going to learn how to salvage a Tuesday at 3:15 PM. We're going to look at why your brain treats a simple task like folding the laundry as a life-threatening predator.

The Only Rule: There is only one rule in this book: **Forgive yourself for the last six hours.** You cannot build a productive future on a foundation of shame. Shame is heavy; it's hard to get anything done when you're lugging it around. So, take a breath. Put down the guilt. You haven't wasted your life; you've just had a very long, very distracted warm-up.

The party is just getting started, and you're exactly on time. Let's get to work (or at least, let's start thinking about starting).

Oh, and can't forgive yourself yet? That's okay, let's deep dive it.

PART 1: WHY WE'RE ALWAYS SHOWING UP FASIONABLY LATE

Chapter 1: You're Not Lazy, You're Human (The Official Diagnosis)

We toss the word lazy around like it's a verified medical condition. We wear it like a hair shirt, hoping the discomfort of the label will eventually goad us into action. I'm just lazy, we tell our partners, our bosses, and—most damagingly—ourselves.

But here's the secret the high-performance gurus don't want you to know: Lazy doesn't actually exist. Think about it. Have you ever met a truly lazy person? I mean someone who genuinely, deep in their soul, enjoys the feeling of sitting in a pile of unfinished tasks while their anxiety levels redline? No. That's not enjoying rest. That's a hostage situation.

When we call ourselves lazy, we are mislabeling a complex cocktail of fear, over-stimulation, and what I like to call "The Saber-Toothed Spreadsheet." You see, your brain is an ancient piece of hardware running on very modern, very glitchy software. For the last several hundred thousand years, your brain had one job: don't get eaten. It is hardwired to scan the environment for threats. Back in the day, a threat was a leopard in the tall grass. Today, a threat is a 48-row Excel document or a "We need to talk" email from your manager.

When you look at that to-do list and suddenly find yourself researching the mating habits of flightless birds, you aren't being lazy. You are experiencing a limbic system hijack. Your Amygdala—that tiny, almond-shaped part of your brain responsible for "fight or flight"—has looked at your priority one task and decided it's a predator. And because you can't fight a spreadsheet and you can't exactly run away from your own office chair, your brain chooses the third option: freeze.

You aren't doing nothing. You are stuck in a high-speed spin-cycle of internal panic. You are freezing by scrolling. You are fleeing by cleaning the microwave. You are fighting by picking a fight with someone on Twitter about the ending of the latest movie you saw.

By reframing laziness as biological self-defense mechanism, we can finally stop the shame-spiral. You aren't a broken human being. You are a functional human being with a very confused security system.

The "Not-Lazy" Diagnostic: What Kind of Human Are You?

Before we can fix the engine, we have to pop the hood and see which particular wire is sparking. Because "I can't get anything done" is a broad symptom, but the reason behind it varies.

Below is a highly scientific* (read: I wrote this while eating a cold taco) diagnostic to help you identify your specific brand of "humanity."

*note: not really scientifically proven, but effective nonetheless.

Category 1: The Serial Architect (The Over-Planner)

You don't just have a to-do list; you have a multi-layered, color-coded, cross-referenced system involving three different apps, two physical journals, and a pack of highlighters that cost more than your first car.

The Symptom: You spend four hours onboarding yourself into a new productivity system, only to abandon it the moment you actually have to do a task.

The Saboteur: Your brain thinks that planning the work is the same thing as doing the work. You get a dopamine hit from the font choice on your calendar, but you haven't actually opened the spreadsheet.

The Motto: "I'll start as soon as I find the perfect Tuesday-specific sticker for my planner."

Category 2: The Shiny Object Specialist (The Distraction-Seeker)

You have the best of intentions, but your focus is like a goldfish on an espresso bender. You sit down to write an email and forty minutes later you're watching a documentary on how they make those tiny umbrellas for tropical drinks.

The Symptom: You have 42 open tabs, and at least three of them are playing music you can't locate.

The Saboteur: Your Amygdala is bored. It views deep work as a slow death and new information as a survival requirement. You aren't distracted; you're an information forager who forgot what they were looking for.

The Motto: "Wait, did I just spend an hour looking up the net worth of the kid from *The Sixth Sense*?"

Category 3: The "All-or-Nothing" Astronaut (The Perfectionist)

If you can't do it perfectly, you'd rather set the whole project on fire and walk away in slow motion. You believe that "Good Enough" is a personal insult to your ancestors.

The Symptom: You've already wasted half the day because you missed your 8:00 AM start time by six minutes, so you decided the entire Tuesday is a write-off.

The Saboteur: Your manager brain is a tyrant. It would rather stay at the starting line than risk finishing with a B-minus performance.

The Motto: "If the vibes aren't 100% immaculate, I am legally prohibited from being productive."

Category 4: The Firefighter (The Crisis-Junkie)

You are physically incapable of starting a task unless the deadline is currently screaming in your face and the metaphorical building is already half-engulfed in flames.

The Symptom: You thrive on pressure, which is just a fancy way of saying you live in a constant state of cortisol-soaked terror.

The Saboteur: Your Prefrontal Cortex has a very high boredom threshold. It literally doesn't believe a task is real until there are immediate, painful consequences for not doing it.

The Motto: "I have three hours until the deadline. This is where the magic happens (and by magic, I mean a mild panic attack)."

SELF-IDENTIFICATION TIME

(I am going to upset you, because you'll soon realize we all mostly do the same stuff and need to hear mostly the same sentence in different ways.)

If you identified with Category 3, I have some news for you, and you're probably not going to like it: Your high standards are actually a very sophisticated form of cowardice. *I mean let's be honest, I will go through the different categories, but you are probably mad I started with Category 3 first, instead of chronological order… actually, I am pretty mad about it too. But here we are, and like this book says, I want to stop thinking and start doing…if you're Category 1, you are also probably just as mad…*

14

I know, I know. That stung. Take a minute. Drink some of that lukewarm coffee.

We call it having a commitment to excellence. We tell people, "I just want to do it right." But in the dark, messy corners of our brains, perfectionism is actually just a suit of armor we wear to protect ourselves from the terrifying possibility of being average.

The All-or-Nothing Astronaut lives in a world of binary code: 0 or 1. Success or Failure. Immaculate or Trash. There is no "pretty good" in the Astronaut's vocabulary. If the morning meditation didn't happen, if the breakfast wasn't artisanal, or if—heaven forbid—you started your work block at 9:07 AM instead of the mathematically superior 9:00 AM, the mission is scrubbed.

The Anatomy of a Scrubbed Mission: Let's look at how this plays out in the wild. It's 10:30 AM. You were supposed to start your deep work ninety minutes ago. But you got caught in a spiral of answering just one more trivial email, or perhaps you spent too long choosing the perfect Spotify playlist for "focusing like a boss."

A normal person might say, "Well, I'm ninety minutes late. I'll just start now and do what I can."

But the Astronaut? The Astronaut looks at those ninety lost minutes and sees a catastrophic system failure. To the Astronaut, the integrity of the day has been compromised.

Starting now would feel like wearing a tuxedo with sneakers—it's ruined.

So, instead of starting at 10:31 AM, the Astronaut decides to wait for the next clean break. Maybe 11:00 AM? No, 11:00 is too close to lunch. Let's say 1:00 PM. But then 1:00 PM rolls around and you're in a "food coma" from that burrito, so you push it to tomorrow.

And just like that, you've traded a slightly imperfect Tuesday for a completely non-existent one.

The Immaculate Vibes Fallacy: The reason we do this is that we've romanticized productivity. we think it requires a specific state of being. We wait for the vibe to be right. We wait for the house to be silent, the desk to be clear, and our internal motivation to be at a roaring 10 out of 10.

Here is my reality check: **The "perfect" time to start does not exist.** It is a mirage. It is a carrot on a stick held by a very mean donkey.

If you only work when the conditions are perfect, you will work about three days a year. The rest of the time, you'll be sitting on the launchpad, waiting for the weather to clear while your competitors (who are perfectly happy to fly in a bit of rain) are already orbiting the moon.

The Solution: Lowering the Bar (Until It's on the Floor)

To survive as an Astronaut, you have to learn the art of the scrappy start. We need to redefine what a "successful" day looks like. A successful day isn't one where you checked off 25 items and ran a 5k before sunrise. A successful day is one where you felt like a total mess, realized it was already 2:00 PM, and decided to do one productive thing anyway.

Doing something poorly at 2:15 PM is infinitely more productive than doing nothing perfectly all day long.

If you identified with Category 1, I know exactly what you're doing right now. You've probably already highlighted three sentences in this chapter using a specific color that denotes mindset shifts, and you're currently wondering if I'm going to provide a downloadable, 42-page PDF workbook at the end of this book. (Spoilers: I might, but you'll probably just save it to a folder named "To Process" and never look at it again.)

I know, I know. That stung. Take a minute. Adjust your ergonomically perfect chair. Have a sip of that artisanal water. (Told you we all need to hear the same thing just in different ways).

We call it "being organized." We tell people, "I just need the right tools to be successful." But in the dark, messy corners of our brains, over-planning is actually just a very sophisticated defense mechanism used to avoid the terrifying risk of actually starting.

The Serial Architect lives in a world of blueprints and scaffolding. You are addicted to a very specific, very dangerous drug: The Illusion of Progress.

The Anatomy of the "The Over-Planner" Spiral: Let's look at how this plays out in the wild. It's 10:30 AM. You have a massive project due. A normal person might just open a blank document and start typing "The" over and over again until an idea forms.

But the Architect? The Architect decides that before the work can begin, the environment must be optimized. You spend forty-five minutes researching "The Best Minimalist Task Manager for 2026." You find one. It has beautiful rounded corners and a "dark mode" that makes you feel like a hacker in a movie. You spend the next hour onboarding yourself, importing your tasks, setting up custom tags like #Urgent and #LifeChanging, and choosing a font that inspires creativity.

By the time the system is ready, it's 12:45 PM. You feel incredibly organized. You feel professional. You feel like a person who has their life together. The only problem is that you haven't actually done a single second of the work you were supposed to do.

The Stationery Aisle Fallacy: The reason we do this is that planning is a controlled environment. In a planner, your goals are beautiful and unblemished. In your mind, the project is a masterpiece. The moment you actually start doing the work, however, reality hits. The words are clunky. The spreadsheet has errors. The magic disappears and is replaced by the grind.

The Architect stays in the planning phase because as long as you're still organizing, you haven't failed yet. You've traded the messy reality of a finished project for the clean fantasy of a perfect plan.

The Solution: The "Ugly" Workflow: To survive as an Architect, you have to learn the art of the "Minimum Viable Tool." We need to strip away the bells and whistles.

If you are a writer, your system should be a blinking cursor. If you are a designer, it's a blank canvas. My reality check is this: If you can't get the work done with a scrap of paper and a chewed-up ballpoint pen, a $50-a-month subscription service isn't going to save you.

Doing the work in a boring, ugly way at 2:15 PM is infinitely more productive than spending all day building a shrine of productivity that remains empty.

If you identified with Category 2, I'm honestly impressed you've made it this far into the chapter without being hijacked by a notification for a "limited time offer" on ergonomic footrests or a sudden, burning need to know if you can grow a mulberry tree in a suburban backyard.

If you are still here, stay with me. I'll keep this quick before your brain decides that the texture of the ceiling is suddenly the most fascinating thing in the room.

We call it curiosity. We tell people, "I just have a thirst for knowledge." But in the dark, messy corners of our brains, the Shiny Object Specialist isn't a seeker of truth—you're a Novelty Addict.

The Anatomy of a Hijacked Afternoon: The Specialist doesn't struggle with "starting" (like the Astronaut) or "organizing" (like the Architect). You struggle with "staying." Your brain is essentially a high-speed browser with forty-seven tabs open, and at least three of them are playing a song you can't locate.

Let's look at how the Specialist wastes half the day. It's 11:15 AM. You are supposed to be drafting a project proposal. You need to check one simple fact—let's say, the current population of Brisbane.

You open Google. You see a headline: "Scientists Discover Why Tropical Birds Are So Colorful."

11:20 AM: You are reading about structural coloration in feathers.

11:45 AM: You are on a forum for amateur ornithologists, debating whether a specific type of parrot can actually understand the concept of zero.

12:10 PM: You are researching the cost of flight lessons because, suddenly, your soul demands to be in the sky.

It is now 12:45 PM. You still don't know the population of Brisbane, but you do know that a parrot named Alex once asked what color he was. You've traded your priority one task for a pocketful of knowledge pebbles that have absolutely no bearing on your actual life.

The "Information Forager" Trap: The reason this is so hard to fight is that your brain thinks it's doing something useful. Evolutionarily speaking, your ancestors survived because they noticed the "New" movement in the tall grass. But in the modern world, your "movement in the grass" is a red notification bubble.

Your Amygdala views deep work as a slow, boring death. It views new information as a survival requirement. You aren't lazy; you're a Hunter-Gatherer who has been trapped in a library. You are collecting data for a future that never arrives.

The Solution: The "Parking Lot" and the "Analog Leash": To survive as a Specialist, you have to treat your brain like a hyperactive puppy. You can't just tell it to "Sit" for eight hours; it will lose its mind.

- The "Interesting" Parking Lot: You need a physical notebook where you write down every "Shiny Object" that tries to hijack you. "Can you grow mulberries in the Sahara Dessert? Great question. Write it down. Look it up at 5:00 PM." Once it's on the paper, your brain feels "safe" letting go of the thought.

- The Analog Leash: When you need to do the "Hard Thing," you must create a vacuum of novelty. Turn off the Wi-Fi. Put the phone in another room. If you give yourself a choice between "The Spreadsheet" and "Literally Anything Else on the Internet," the internet will win every single time.

Being a Specialist isn't a flaw; it's a superpower that has been mismanaged. We just need to keep you on the leash long enough to finish the proposal before you fly off to the Amazon.

If you identified with Category 4, I'm going to assume you're reading this while procrastinating on something that is due in approximately three hours. Your heart rate is slightly elevated, you've had four cups of coffee, and you are currently operating on a level of "focused panic" that would make a fighter pilot nervous.

Welcome. Take a breath. (Seriously, breathe. Your shoulders are touching your ears.)

The Firefighter is a unique breed. You don't have a normal gear. You have two settings: catatonic and emergency. When a deadline is three weeks away, it doesn't exist. It is a ghost. It is a whisper in a hurricane. But the moment that deadline hits the red zone? You become a god.

The Cortisol High: The Firefighter is addicted to the most dangerous drug in the productivity world: Stress. You've convinced yourself of a very specific lie: "I actually do my best work under pressure." Let's be honest—that's not best work; that's survival work. You've conditioned your Prefrontal Cortex to only wake up when the "Fear Center" (the Amygdala) starts screaming that your career/reputation/life is about to end.

Because your executive function is a bit of a slacker, it needs a giant spike of cortisol and adrenaline to actually start the engine. You don't move for internal motivation. You only move for imminent consequences.

The Anatomy of a "Last-Minute Miracle": Let's look at your "Wasted Half-Day." It's 10:00 AM. You have a report due at 5:00 PM.

10:00 AM – 2:00 PM: You do nothing. You stare at the screen. You clean the microwave. You research the best way to descale a kettle. You feel a vague, growing sense of dread, but you can't seem to make your fingers type.

2:15 PM: The Panic hits. The fire has started.

2:16 PM – 4:59 PM: You are a blur of activity. You are typing at 120 words per minute. You are synthesizing data like a supercomputer. You aren't even blinking.

5:00 PM: You hit 'Send.' You are exhausted, your eyes are twitching, and you feel a strange sense of triumph.

But here is the reality check: You aren't a hero for putting out a fire that you started yourself.

The Solution: The "Controlled Burn": The Firefighter is late to their own life because they spend the first half of every day waiting for the panic to arrive. You are effectively holding yourself hostage. To survive as a Firefighter, we have to stop relying on the Big Inferno. We have to learn how to create Artificial Small Fires.

- The Public Deadline: Tell someone you'll show them a draft by 2:00 PM. The fear of looking like a flake to them will kick-start your brain earlier than the fear of the actual deadline.

- The "Sprint" Timer: Set a timer for 15 minutes and tell yourself you only have to work until it beeps. For a Firefighter, a "ticking clock" is the only language the brain understands.

Living in a constant state of crisis management is a fast track to burnout. We want to move you from emergency responder to consistent human.

The "Shame-Stripping" Finale: Embracing Your Messy Humanity

If you've just spent the last few pages nodding along and feeling a strange mixture of "I've been seen" and "I've been personally attacked," congratulations. You've officially been diagnosed.

Whether you're an Astronaut waiting for the perfect vibes, an Architect building a cathedral of to-do lists, a Specialist chasing digital butterflies, or a Firefighter who only moves when the building is screaming—here is the truth: You are not broken. You are a functional human being with a very confused, very ancient security system.

The "Hybrid" Confession: I'll let you in on a secret: I am not just one of these. I am a "Specialist Architect." That is a particularly dangerous cocktail where I spend three hours building a beautiful, color-coded spreadsheet (Architect) specifically so I can use it to track my "research" into whether or not I could survive a zombie apocalypse in suburbia (Specialist).

I have wasted more Tuesdays than I can count. I have sat in the wreckage of a scrubbed mission at 4:00 PM, feeling like a massive failure.

But here is what I learned, and what I want you to tattoo on the inside of your eyelids: Shame is the ultimate productivity killer. When you sit in the guilt of a wasted morning, you aren't reflecting. You are dragging a giant, heavy anchor behind you while trying to run a marathon. You cannot build a productive afternoon on a foundation of self-loathing. It doesn't work. It's like trying to start a car by screaming at the engine—it might make you feel like you're doing something, but the car isn't moving an inch.

The First Tiny Rebellion: As we close this chapter and prepare to dive into the "Half-Day Trap" in Chapter 2, I want to give you your first assignment. It's not a 12-step program. It's not a morning routine involving kale and ice baths.

It's a Tiny Rebellion.

Your assignment is this: Forgive yourself for the last six hours. Literally. Say it out loud if you have to (preferably not in a crowded cafe, but hey, you do you). Acknowledge that you were an Astronaut, or a Firefighter, or whatever label fit. And then, let it go.

We are going to stop trying to be "The Person Who Never Wastes Time." That person doesn't exist. They are a myth created by people trying to sell you expensive planners. Instead, we are going to become "The Person Who Recovers Quickly."

The party isn't over just because you showed up late. The second half of the day is still waiting for you. It doesn't care that you spent the morning looking at parrot videos. It just wants to know what you're going to do now.

Take a breath. Drink the rest of that cold coffee (or better yet, get a fresh one).

Chapter 2: The Half-Day Trap (Why Mornings Feel Infinite and Afternoons Vanish Like Socks in the Dryer)

If you were to look at a clock at 8:00 AM, you would see a vast, shimmering ocean of possibility. Eight hours. Four hundred and eighty minutes. Twenty-eight thousand, eight hundred seconds.

At 8:00 AM, you are a Time Billionaire. When you have that much currency in your pocket, you become incredibly reckless with your spending. You tell yourself, "I've got all day. I'll just spend twenty minutes seeing what's trending on Twitter. It's fine. I'll still have seven hours and forty minutes left. That's basically an eternity." Then you spend another fifteen minutes clearing the decks – which is the professional-sounding term we use for unsubscribing from newsletters we never signed up for and deleting blurry photos of our own feet from our camera rolls.

You treat the morning like a bottomless well. You assume that the "Future You" who exists at 2:00 PM is going to be a highly disciplined, caffeinated version of a Navy SEAL who can effortlessly crush a mountain of work in a single sitting.

But then, the "Half-Day Trap" springs its leak. You look up from a quick deep-dive into the history of competitive cheese-rolling, and suddenly, the clock says 1:47 PM. The vast ocean of the morning has evaporated, leaving behind nothing but a salty puddle of regret and a low-battery notification on your laptop.

This is where the "Temporal Mirage" hits its peak. In the morning, an hour feels like a week. In the afternoon, an hour feels like a sneeze.

Why does this happen? Why is it that we can spend four hours preparing to work and feel like we've barely started, but when we finally sit down to do the actual task, the sun immediately starts to set and the crows begin to circle?

It's because we are victims of a biological and psychological heist. We've been robbed, not by laziness, but by a set of universal glitches in the human operating system that make us treat time like a renewable resource, when in reality, it's a melting ice cube in a hot car.

If the morning is a "Temporal Mirage," the afternoon is a biological "Black Hole." Most productivity gurus tell you that the afternoon slump is a sign of weakness. They suggest that if you just had more grit, or perhaps a higher-quality MCT oil in your coffee, you wouldn't feel like a human sloth at 2:30 PM. But I'm here to tell you that your afternoon fatigue isn't a character flaw—it's a pre-programmed system update that you didn't ask for and can't opt out of.

The "Decision Token" Theory: Imagine that every morning when you wake up, the Universe hands you a small leather pouch containing fifty gold "Decision

Tokens." These tokens are your currency for willpower, focus, and executive function. In the morning, you feel rich. You spend your tokens recklessly.

Token 1: Deciding which shirt to wear.

Token 2: Deciding whether to have toast or a smoothie.

Token 3: Deciding which route to take to work to avoid that one specific construction zone.

By the time you actually sit down at your desk at 9:00 AM, you've already spent ten tokens, but you don't care because you've still got forty left. You feel like a high-roller. You spend tokens on "checking Slack," "replying to a trivial text," and "deciding which font to use for your to-do list."

But here is the catch: Your brain doesn't distinguish between a "Big Decision" and a "Tiny Decision." Choosing the wording of a million-dollar contract costs one token. Choosing whether to use a blue or black pen also costs one token. By 1:30 PM, you reach into your pouch and realize... you're down to your last three coins.

This is the scientific reality of Decision Fatigue. Your Prefrontal Cortex—the "CEO" of your brain—is an energy-hungry diva. It requires a massive amount of glucose and oxygen to function. By early afternoon, the CEO has gone on an unannounced liquid lunch and left the "Intern" (your Limbic System) in charge.

The Intern doesn't want to do hard things. The Intern wants to look at memes. The Intern wants to know if that actor from that one show in the 90s is still alive. When you try to force yourself to work at 2:00 PM with zero tokens left, you aren't just fighting "laziness"; you're trying to buy a Ferrari with a pocketful of lint.

The Post-Prandial Dip: The "Food Coma" is Real

Then, we have to talk about the "Burrito Factor." Around 1:00 PM, most of us engage in a ritual called lunch. Whether it's a sophisticated salad or a questionable microwave burrito, the biological result is the same: your body diverts its resources away from your brain and toward your digestive system.

This is the Post-Prandial Dip. It is a natural part of the human circadian rhythm. Even if you didn't eat lunch, your body's internal clock is programmed to have a "low energy" window in the early afternoon. In many cultures, this is called "Siesta Time." In our culture, it's called "Staring Blankly at an Outlook Calendar While Questioning Your Life Choices."

Trying to do deep work during the Dip is like trying to drive a car with no oil in the engine. You might get a few miles down the road, but the screeching sound you hear is your brain grinding to a halt. The "Half-Day Trap" isn't just about time; it's about the fact that your biological operating system is currently running a background scan that is taking up 90% of your CPU.

Attention Residue: The Ghost in the Machine: But wait, it gets worse! (I promise this gets positive eventually, but we have to understand the disaster before we can clean it up.)

There is a phenomenon called Attention Residue, coined by Dr Sophie Leroy. It's the idea that when you switch from Task A to Task B, a "residue" of your attention stays stuck on Task A.

Think of your attention like a roll of high-quality duct tape. Every time you "quickly check" an email or "glance" at a notification, you're sticking that tape onto a new surface and then ripping it off. By 2:00 PM, your "Attention Tape" is covered in dog hair, dust, and tiny fragments of fifty different half-finished thoughts. It's not sticky anymore. It won't hold anything together.

When you look at your priority one task in the afternoon, your brain is still processing that weirdly passive-aggressive comment your mother-in-law made on Facebook three hours ago, and that one email about the "Urgent Meeting" that ended up being a waste of time.

You aren't multitasking. You're just leave-taking— leaving bits of your soul in every browser tab you opened this morning.

The "Sunk Cost" Afternoon: The Psychology of the Write-Off. Finally, we hit the psychological wall.

By the time you've navigated Decision Fatigue, the Post-Prandial Dip, and Attention Residue, you look at the clock. It's 2:45 PM.

In your head, you have a model day. In this model, you are productive from 9:00 to 5:00. Because you've already failed the first five hours, your brain engages in a cognitive bias called The Sunk Cost Fallacy. You think: "Well, the day is 60% over and I haven't done anything. The 'integrity' of the day is ruined. There's no point starting now because I won't finish anyway. I'll just 'prep' for tomorrow and start fresh."

This is the equivalent of dropping your phone, seeing a tiny scratch on the screen, and then stomping on it with a work boot because "it's already broken."

It's completely irrational. Three hours of work is still three hours of work. But to the "Half-Day" brain, those three hours feel like a consolation prize that we don't even want to accept. We would rather have a perfect zero than a messy fifty percent.

If you've ever dropped your phone on the pavement, seen a single spider-web crack in the corner, and felt a strange, dark impulse to just throw the whole thing against a brick wall because "it's already ruined," then you understand the Sunk Cost Afternoon.

In economics, the "Sunk Cost Fallacy" is the phenomenon where humans continue an endeavor as a result of previously invested resources (time, money, or effort), even if the current costs outweigh the benefits. In productivity, it's much simpler: It's the belief that if you've "failed" the morning, the afternoon is a write-off.

The Math of the "Wasted" Tuesday: Let's look at the cold, hard mathematics of your despair. Let's say your workday is eight hours long. You start at 9:00 AM. By 1:30 PM, you realize that you have spent four and a half hours doing... well, not much. You've checked your email fourteen times, you've read a long-form article about the decline of the Roman Empire, and you've spent twenty minutes trying to remember the name of that actor who was in that one movie with the guy from the other thing. At 1:30 PM, your brain does a quick calculation:

Time Invested: 4.5 hours.

Result: Zero.

Efficiency: 0%.

To your logical brain, the remaining three and a half hours are still three and a half hours of pure, unadulterated potential. You could write two thousand words. You could finish that spreadsheet. You could literally change the trajectory of your week.

But your emotional brain—the one currently wearing a "I'm With Stupid" t-shirt—sees it differently. It sees a perfect day that has been tainted. To the emotional brain, those remaining hours aren't an opportunity; they are a consolation prize. And nobody wants a consolation prize. We would rather have a grand failure than a mediocre recovery.

The "Clean Slate" Addiction: The reason the "Half-Day Trap" is so effective is that humans are addicted to clean slates. We love the idea of a fresh start. It's why we start diets on Mondays, why we make New Year's Resolutions, and why we wait until the clock hits a "Round Number" (like 2:00 PM or 3:00 PM) to start a task. If it's 2:04 PM, we feel like we've "missed the window," so we wait until 3:00 PM to maintain the integrity of the hour.

This is the Immaculate Vibes Fallacy. We believe that productivity requires a specific energy that only exists at the beginning of a fresh unit of time.

The Sunk Cost Afternoon is a "Self-Fulfilling Prophecy." You feel like you've wasted the day, so you spend the rest of the day actually wasting it to prove yourself right. You lean into the failure. You decide that since you're already behind, you might as well stay behind and start fresh tomorrow.

But tomorrow is just another Tuesday in a trench coat. Tomorrow will have its own distractions, its own "Post-Prandial Dips," and its own Wikipedia rabbit holes.

The "Cracked Screen" Realization: The reality check for the Sunk Cost Afternoon is this: A cracked screen still works. If you drop your phone and it gets a scratch, you don't throw it in the river. You keep using it. You make calls, you send texts, and you eventually forget the scratch is even there.

Your day is the same way. A wasted morning is just a scratch on the screen of your week. It's not a total system failure. The afternoon doesn't need to be immaculate to be effective.

We need to stop waiting for the clean slate and start getting comfortable with the dirty start. We need to realize that 50% of a workday is infinitely better than 0%. In fact, in the world of productivity for people like us, a salvaged Tuesday is actually a greater achievement than a perfect Monday, because it required you to defeat your own ego to get it done.

If you were to walk into a physical bank and see a group of people systematically emptying the vault into duffel bags, you'd call the police. You'd be outraged. You'd recognize it as a high-stakes robbery.

Yet, every single Tuesday at approximately 11:14 AM, we allow a group of Silicon Valley engineers to walk into the "Vault of Our Afternoon" and walk out with our most precious currency—our attention—and we don't even put up a fight. In fact, we usually invite them in. We open the door, offer them a metaphorical biscuit, and say, "I'll just check this one thing. It'll only take five minutes."

This is the "Just Five Minutes" Lie. It is the single most destructive sentence in the modern world. It is the gateway drug to the Half-Day Trap.

To understand why five minutes always turns into forty-five, we have to look at the Variable Reward Schedule. This is a fancy psychological term for a slot machine.

When you pull the lever on a slot machine, you don't know if you're going to get three cherries or a handful of nothing. That uncertainty is exactly what keeps you sitting there until your legs go numb. Your brain loves the "maybe."

Your smartphone is a portable, high-definition slot machine.

The Email Refresh: Pull the lever. Maybe it's a million-dollar contract. (It's usually a Groupon for a colonic.)

The Instagram Scroll: Pull the lever. Maybe someone liked your photo of that lukewarm laksa.

The News Feed: Pull the lever. Maybe the world ended while you were in the shower.

When you say, "I'll just check my notifications for five minutes," you aren't "checking." You are gambling with your focus capital. You are betting that you can pull the lever once and walk away. But the house always wins. The engineers who built these apps spent billions of dollars ensuring that you cannot walk away after one pull. They've turned your quick check into a dopamine binge that leaves your prefrontal cortex hungover and incapable of doing the spreadsheet you actually get paid for.

The "Open Tab" Graveyard (Future-Self Sabotage): Take a look at your browser right now. I'm serious. Count them.

If you have more than seven tabs open, you aren't multitasking. You are hosting an Open Tab Graveyard. Each of those tabs is a future commitment that you haven't had the guts to kill.

Tab 1: A half-read article on "How to fix a leaky faucet" (A hobby you don't have).

Tab 2: An Amazon cart with a pair of noise-canceling headphones (A purchase you can't justify).

Tab 3: A YouTube video titled "10 Habits of Highly Successful People" (The ultimate irony).

Every open tab is a tiny mental leak. Your brain is a processor, and every tab is a background program running in the human OS. Even if you aren't looking at them, your brain is constantly scanning them, whispering: "Don't forget me. You still haven't learned about 18th-century maritime law. You still haven't bought those headphones." By 2:00 PM, your system memory is full. You feel sluggish, not because the work is hard, but because you are mentally carrying twenty-seven potential lives at the same time.

You've cluttered your digital workspace so thoroughly that there's no room left for the actual life you're trying to lead.

This is the most intellectual way we lie to ourselves. We call it due diligence. We call it "Gathering Data."

I call it The Information Horizon. It's the point where "Researching the best flight to Sydney" becomes "Looking at 400 photos of hotel bathrooms in a city you aren't even visiting."

We believe that more information leads to better decisions. But in reality, Information is a Weight. The more you gather, the harder it is to move. The Shiny Object Specialist (Category 2) is the master of this. They spend so much time "preparing" to be productive that they run out of time to actually be productive. They are like a chef who spends eight hours sharpening a knife but never actually chops an onion.

In the morning, when you are a "Time Billionaire," this research feels like an investment. By 3:00 PM, you realize it was actually an Expense. You've traded your "Execution Energy" for "Observation Energy." You know everything about the topic, but you've done nothing about it.

We've all told ourselves this one: "I just finished a hard task. I'll just scroll TikTok for ten minutes to clear my head." This is like saying, "I just finished a workout, I'll just smoke a pack of cigarettes to clear my lungs." Social media is not a palette cleanser. It is Dopamine Napalm. It doesn't "reset" your focus; it incinerates it. When you enter the Infinite Scroll, your brain is bombarded with high-contrast, high-novelty stimuli. You move from a "Deep Work" state (Low stimulation, High focus) to a "Scatter" state (High stimulation, Zero focus).

Once you've "Scattered" your brain, it takes an average of twenty-three minutes to get back into a state of "Flow." So, that "ten-minute break" actually costs you thirty-three minutes of your life. Do that three times a day, and you've just flushed an hour and forty minutes of your "Billionaire" currency down the toilet.

The Architecture of the Rabbit Hole: The modern internet is not a library; it's a labyrinth. It is designed to be easy to enter and impossible to leave.

Every link is a "Shiny Object." Every "Recommended for You" video is a personalized trap. When you say, "I'll just check this one thing," you are stepping into a machine that was built by the smartest people on Earth to ensure you don't do your work.

They don't want you to be a lawyer, a doctor, an entrepreneur. They don't want you to write a 3-book series on productivity. They want you to watch "Top 10 Fails of 2025" so they can sell your attention to an insurance company.

Reality check this: Every "Quick Check" is a transaction. You are selling your future potential for a five-second hit of novelty. Is that trade worth it? Is a video of a dog riding a skateboard worth the "Integrity" of your Tuesday?

Usually, the answer is no. But by the time we realize it, the "Digital Termites" have already eaten the beams of our afternoon, and we're sitting in the rubble wondering where the day went.

Here's the good news buried under all this wreckage: The afternoon isn't gone until you decide it is. The Half-Day Trap only wins if you let it declare the entire day a write-off. But you can flip the script. You can declare Salvage Mode at 3:17 PM (or whenever the regret hits peak intensity). Salvage Mode doesn't require a clean slate, perfect vibes, or a sudden surge of motivation. It just requires one decision: "I'm starting anyway."

Think of it like this: Your morning was the expensive dinner you ordered that turned out to be disappointing. You already paid for it (in time and tokens). But you don't have to throw the rest of the evening away too. You can still enjoy dessert—or at least eat something that doesn't make you hate yourself.

Here are the Tiny Rebellions that actually work when the trap has already sprung (we'll go deeper in Part 2, but let's plant the seeds now):

The 2-Minute Forgiveness Reset

Say it out loud or in your head: "The morning happened. It's over. I forgive it. What's one thing I can do right now?". This isn't woo-woo positivity; it's neurological. Shame keeps the Amygdala on high alert. Forgiveness dials it down so your Prefrontal Cortex (the actual adult in the room) can get back online.

The "One Stupid Thing" Rule

Pick the dumbest, smallest version of your most important task. Not "finish the report"—just "open the document and type one sentence." Not "clean the kitchen"—just "put one dish in the sink." Momentum is physics, not motivation. Once the object is in motion, it's easier to keep it going. Your brain hates unfinished open loops more than it hates starting.

The Analog Escape

Close every tab. Put the phone face-down in another room. Grab a scrap of paper or a notebook (the uglier, the better—no fancy journals allowed). Write down the one thing you're going to do for the next 15 minutes. Set a timer. When the digital slot machine is offline, your brain has no choice but to deal with reality. It's brutal at first, but it's also liberating.

The Post-Slump Micro-Win Stack

After your first small win, stack another tiny one immediately. Celebrate nothing. No big self-high-five—just chain them. One sentence becomes one paragraph becomes one section. One dish becomes half the sink. This rebuilds your Decision Tokens faster than caffeine or sugar ever could.

The "Cracked Screen" Mantra

Repeat after me: "A scratched screen still works." Your day has a dent. Fine. It still functions. You don't need to factory-reset your life every Tuesday. You just need to keep using it.

The Afternoon Isn't a Write-Off—It's a Redemption Arc

The Half-Day Trap thrives on the illusion that productivity is all-or-nothing. But real life isn't a perfect Monday montage; it's a series of messy recoveries. The people who "have it together" aren't the ones who never fall into the trap—they're the ones who climb out fastest.

You don't need to win the morning to win the day. You just need to refuse to let the morning win.

So, if it's 3:42 PM and you're reading this with cold coffee and a vague sense of doom—congratulations. You're exactly where most of us live. The trap has you in its jaws, but the jaws are surprisingly loose.

Take one breath. Forgive the last six hours (or eight, or whatever).

Pick one stupid thing. Start. The second half is yours. It's not perfect. It's not pretty. But it's available. And that's enough.

PART 2: THE TOOLKIT – TINY REBELLIONS THAT ACTUALLY STICK

Chapter 3: The 5-Minute Rebellion (Because Starting Is The Hardest Part… and Also the Easiest to Fake)

If Chapters 1 and 2 were the part where we held up a mirror and said, "Yep, that's why your Tuesdays keep evaporating," then this chapter is where we finally hand you a small, slightly chipped hammer and say, "Okay, let's smash something useful with this."

Welcome to the 5-Minute Rebellion—the first real weapon in the Tiny Rebellions arsenal. It's not flashy. It's not complicated. It doesn't require a new app, a color-coded journal, or waking up at dawn to chant affirmations to your houseplants. It's just five minutes. And that's exactly why it works when everything else has failed you for years.

Let's be brutally honest for a second: the single biggest wall between you and literally anything you want to accomplish isn't talent, time, energy, or even motivation. It's the act of starting.

Starting feels like walking into a dark room where anything could be waiting. Your ancient brain—still running on software that was last updated during the Pleistocene—sees "beginning a task" as high-risk behavior. What if there's a predator? What if it hurts? What if you embarrass yourself? What if you waste energy on something that doesn't pay off? Better to stay frozen, scanning for threats, than to commit to movement.

That freeze response isn't laziness. It's survival math that's hilariously outdated in 2026. Your "threat" is a blank Google Doc, a tax form PDF, or a pile of laundry that's starting to develop its own personality. But the Amygdala doesn't care about context. It just screams DANGER and slams on the brakes.

Most productivity advice tries to bulldoze that wall: "Just do it!" "Push through the resistance!" "Visualize success!" All of which sounds great until you're sitting there at 3:14 p.m. with zero forward motion and a growing sense that you're constitutionally defective.

The 5-Minute Rebellion doesn't bulldoze the wall. It walks up, knocks politely, and says, "Hey, I'm just gonna peek inside for five minutes. If it's awful, I'll leave forever. Promise."

Your brain—desperate for any escape from the guilt loop—usually says yes. Because five minutes is laughably small. It's shorter than the average TikTok doom-scroll session. It's less time than it takes to make mediocre instant coffee. It's so tiny that refusing it would feel more ridiculous than doing it. And that's the magic.

The Contract: Five Minutes, Full Exit Clause.

Here's how you make the deal official: Pick the task you've been avoiding. Any task. Doesn't matter how big or small. Writing the novel, replying to that awkward email, folding the mountain of clothes, starting the side hustle spreadsheet, calling your accountant, whatever.

Shrink it to its most pathetic, lowest-friction, most embarrassing possible version. Examples:

Not "write chapter 3." → "Open Scrivener/Word/Notepad and type one sentence. Even if it's 'This is stupid and I hate everything.'"

Not "go for a 5 km run." → "Put on running shoes and walk to the end of the driveway. That's it."

Not "deep clean the kitchen." → "Stand in the kitchen and wash one single fork."

Not "meditate properly." → "Sit on the floor and breathe in for four counts, out for four, five times. No app, no candles, no zen playlist."

Set a real, physical timer for five minutes. Not your phone (we'll get to why phones are traitors in Chapter 6). Use the microwave, the oven timer, a cheap kitchen egg timer, the stopwatch on your ancient sports watch—anything that ticks audibly and can't be silently dismissed with a swipe.

Say the contract out loud or in your head (saying it out loud helps more than you think):

"I'm only doing this for five minutes. When the timer goes off, I can stop forever. No guilt. No shame. I'm allowed to quit and go back to doom-scrolling guilt-free. Deal?"

Hit start. Go.

When the beep happens? Stop. Walk away. Drink water. Stare at the wall. Tell yourself, "I kept my promise to myself. That's enough." … Except… almost nobody actually stops.

Why Almost Nobody Stops (The Brain Tricks That Backfire Beautifully): There are three interlocking psychological mechanisms that turn your five-minute fake-out into real progress:

The Zeigarnik Effect (The Open-Loop Itch): In the late 1920s, psychologist Bluma Zeigarnik observed something odd while watching waiters in a café: they remembered unfinished orders perfectly, but forgot completed ones the moment the bill was paid.

Your brain hates open loops. An unfinished task creates cognitive tension—like a background program that won't stop pinging. When you commit to only five minutes, you're not "starting the scary big thing." You're just cracking open a tiny, harmless loop. Once it's open, your mind starts nagging: "Hey... you didn't finish that. It's still hanging there. Close it?"

The tension is uncomfortable enough that continuing often feels easier than walking away.

Activation Energy + Momentum Physics: Borrow a concept from chemistry: every reaction needs a minimum "activation energy" to get going. Ice doesn't melt until you hit 0°C. Matches don't light until you apply enough friction.

Big tasks have huge activation energy walls. "Write the report" requires mental prep, emotional courage, environmental setup, fear management—the works. But "type one stupid sentence" has almost zero activation energy. It's a speed bump, not a cliff.

Once you're past the bump, Newton's first law kicks in: an object in motion stays in motion. You're already typing, so adding another sentence costs almost nothing. The friction is gone. Momentum carries you.

Sunk-Cost Fallacy (Finally Working in Your Favor): Normally this bias screws you: you stay in bad movies because "I already paid for the ticket." But here it flips. After five minutes you've invested something—five minutes of your life, a tiny bit of identity ("I'm someone who follows through"). Quitting now feels like wasting that investment. So the brain whispers, "Might as well keep going... we're already here."

Put those three together and five minutes becomes fifteen, becomes forty-five, becomes "holy crap I just did two hours of the thing I've been avoiding for three weeks."

Real(ish) Stories from People Who've Tried This (Including Me)

Let's make this less theoretical.

My First 5-Minute Rebellion (The Book You're Reading)

I wrote roughly 40% of this manuscript between 2 p.m. and 5 p.m. on various "wasted" afternoons. The pattern was always the same: I'd be staring at a blank page, convinced I had nothing left to say. I'd set the timer for five minutes with the promise I could delete everything afterward. First sentence: "This feels pointless." Second: "But I'm already typing, so whatever." By the beep I usually had 200–300 words. I kept going because stopping felt dumber than continuing. That's how a book about being late to your own life got finished mostly in the afternoons.

Sarah, the Tax Procrastinator:

A friend (name changed, obviously) had three years of unfiled business receipts. Every January she'd panic, then freeze. One April afternoon she set five minutes to "just open the folder on her desktop." She opened it. Saw the mess. Felt sick. Timer beeped. She stopped… for about ninety seconds. Then thought, "I already looked at it. Might as well move one receipt to the 'scanned' folder."

Two hours later she'd scanned sixty documents and felt like she'd won the lottery. She finished the backlog over the next three weekends using chained five-minute blocks.

Jake, the Guy Who "Hates Exercise":

Jake hadn't worked out consistently since high school. His rebellion: five minutes to "just put on gym shorts and stand in the living room." He did it. Felt stupid. Timer went off. He thought, "I already look like an idiot in these shorts. Might as well do five push-ups." Did ten. Then squats. Ended up doing twenty-five minutes. He now uses the "shorts rule" three times a week. The rebellion tricked him into identity change: from "I hate exercise" to "I'm someone who sometimes does exercise."

The Laundry Monster: You know the pile that grows sentient? I set five minutes to "sort only underwear." Ended up doing socks, then shirts, then the whole load because the open loop ("there are still socks on the floor") was more annoying than continuing.

These aren't miracles. They're just what happens when you make starting so small that resistance can't justify itself. The Sneaky Ways Your Brain Will Try to Sabotage (And Counter-Moves). Your mind is clever. It will throw these curveballs during your five minutes:

The Pre-Start Perfection Trap: "I can't start until I have the right notebook / playlist / lighting / emotional state."

Counter: Timer starts now. Work in bad lighting, with silence, using the back of an envelope and a dying pen. Perfection is the enemy of five minutes.

The Mid-Timer Renegotiation: Two minutes in: "This is dumb. I'll do something else first and come back."

Counter: No side quests. The contract is five minutes on this thing. No tea, no quick email, no "just one tab." Those are escape attempts.

The "I Feel Worse Now" Spiral: "See? I started and it still sucks. I'm a failure."

Counter: That's just the resistance lying. Feeling worse for two minutes is still better than feeling guilty for six hours. And the feeling usually passes once momentum builds.

The Legitimate Stop (Rare, But Valid): Timer beeps. You truly, deeply want to quit.

Counter: Quit. Then say out loud: "I kept my promise. That's a win." Log it mentally as evidence you can trust yourself. Next time the contract will feel safer.

How to Scale It Without Turning It Into Another Pressure System

Once five minutes starts working, don't immediately demand hour-long sessions. That's how rebellions die.

Instead: Chain them: Five minutes → 30-second breather (stand up, shake arms) → another five. Repeat. Most people chain 3–6 blocks without noticing.

Habit-stack it: Tie it to an existing ritual. After you finish your coffee → five minutes on the hardest task. After brushing teeth at night → five minutes on tomorrow's planning.

Level up gradually: When five feels automatic, try "10-Minute Rebellion." But only when five stops feeling like a stretch.

Theme days: Monday = admin five-minutes. Wednesday = creative five-minutes. Keeps it playful.

The rule: never make it feel like punishment. The moment it stops being a cheeky trick and starts feeling like boot camp, your brain will mutiny.

Your Assignment (Do It Before You Forget): Right now—yes, while the iron is hot—pick one thing you've been avoiding today or this week.

Name it (in your head or on paper): e.g., "Email to boss about overdue report."

Shrink it: "Open Gmail, type subject line and one sentence."

Grab a real timer (pause reading if needed).

Say the contract: "Five minutes only. Then I can quit forever."

Start.

When it beeps: stop if you want. Keep going if you feel the pull. Either way, you win.

If you stop? You still proved you can make and keep a promise to yourself.

If you keep going? You just stole back part of your day.

That's the rebellion.

This isn't about becoming one of those terrifying 5 a.m. ice-bath people.

It's about becoming someone who can look at 3:47 p.m. on a Thursday, feel the familiar dread, and think: "Fine. Five minutes. Let's see what happens." Because once you fake the start… the real start usually sneaks in behind it.

Chapter 4: The "Three Things" Rule: Chaos-Proofing Your List (Because 47 Items is A "Suicide Mission")

We need to talk about that 47-item list you've got scrawled in your notebook or buried in that "Productivity App" you spent $50 on last month (Or the unopened tabs on your browser. Or the important deadlines you are saving until later… or whatever else you are stashing).

You call it a "To-Do List." I call it a Suicide Mission for your Self-Esteem.

Most people treat their To-Do list like a grocery list for a supermarket that doesn't exist. We keep adding items—fix the website, call the accountant, research 18th-century maritime law, buy milk—as if the mere act of writing them down is a form of progress. We think that if we just list everything, we will somehow become the kind of person who can do everything.

But here is the reality check: Your To-Do list is a liar. It is a document designed to make you feel like a failure before you've even had your first cup of coffee.

The Cognitive Cost of the Infinite List: Remember the Decision Tokens from Chapter 2? Every single item on your list costs you a token just to look at it. When you open your planner and see twenty-five tasks staring back at you, your brain performs a massive, background priority calculation. It tries to weigh the importance of client proposal against order printer ink.

By the time you've finished reading your own list, you've already spent half your mental energy for the morning. You've triggered the Saber-Toothed Spreadsheet response (Chapter 1). Your Amygdala looks at that wall of text, realizes it can't possibly win, and suggests that you go look at real estate listings in a country you don't live in instead.

The infinite list is a form of future-self sabotage. You are writing a contract for a version of "You" that doesn't exist. You're writing it for the heroic you who has infinite energy and no distractions. But the actual you—the one sitting in an office somewhere, or a coffee shop for that matter, with a ringing phone and a full inbox—is the one who has to sign the check. And that person is broke.

The "Closed List" vs. The "Open Wound"

Most people keep "Open Lists." This is a list that never ends. You finish one task, and three more take its place. It's like trying to empty the ocean with a teaspoon. There is no finish Line. There is only the next thing.

This is why we feel the Sunk Cost Slump at 2:00 PM. If the list is infinite, then success is impossible. And if success is impossible, why bother trying?

The "Three Things" Rule is about closing the loop. It's about creating a Closed List. A vault. A tiny, fortress-like plan that protects your focus from the chaos of the world.

The Geometry of Three: Why three? Why not five? Why not one?

One is too fragile. If you pick one thing and get stuck, your whole day is a wash. Five is too heavy. Five things require too many Decision Tokens to manage. Three is the "Golden Ratio" of the human brain.

Three things are enough to feel like a significant victory, but small enough to fit inside your working memory. You can remember three things without looking at a piece of paper. You can hold three things in your head while you're making a coffee. Three things are Human-Sized.

How can "Three" possibly be enough?

It's enough because of the $25,000 Story.

In 1918, Charles M. Schwab—one of the richest men in the world and president of Bethlehem Steel—was obsessed with efficiency. He didn't want his executives to work longer (they were already doing that); he wanted them to work better. He brought in a productivity consultant named Ivy Lee. Lee didn't arrive with a team of analysts or a 400-page manual. He sat down with Schwab and said, "Give me fifteen minutes with each of your executives."

Schwab, ever the businessman, asked, "How much will this cost me?" Lee replied, "Nothing. Unless it works. After three months, you can send me a check for whatever you feel the advice was worth."

The advice Lee gave the executives was deceptively simple:

1. At the end of each day, write down the six most important things you need to accomplish tomorrow. (For our purposes, we are going to be even more radical and say three.)

2. Rank them in order of true importance.

3. Tomorrow morning, start on Task Number One. Do not look at Task Number Two until Task Number One is finished. 4. If you don't finish all six, move the remaining ones to the next day's list.

Three months later, Schwab sent Ivy Lee a check for $25,000. In 1918, that was a king's ransom—roughly $500,000 in today's money. For fifteen minutes of advice.

Why was it worth half a million dollars? Because it solved the Decision Fatigue problem we discussed in Chapter 2. It removed the choice from the workday. When those executives sat down, they didn't have to decide what to do. The decision had already been made by their smarter, yesterday-self. They didn't spend their first two hours clearing the decks or getting organized. They just started.

The "1-2" Geometry: One Big Rock, Two Pebbles: Now, let's be real. For a Recovering Human who has already spent the morning researching the history of the stapler, "Six Things" is still a bit ambitious. It invites the "Sunk Cost" ghost to the party. We are going to simplify the geometry further with the 1-2 Structure.

The "One" (The Big Rock): This is your High-Value Task (HVT). It's the task that actually moves the needle on your revenue or your case. It's the one that makes your stomach do a tiny flip when you think about it. If you get this done, the day is a Success, even if you do literally nothing else. It's writing the closing argument; it's making the "Big Ask" to a major lead.

The "Two" (The Pebbles): These are the "Maintenance" tasks. They are necessary, but they don't require your peak cognitive brilliance. Paying an overdue invoice, sending a brief update to a client, or checking a specific legal precedent. They require fewer "Decision Tokens," but they need to happen to keep the wheels from falling off.

When you look at a list of three, your brain doesn't see a "Suicide Mission"; it sees a Game.

The "Win-Rate" and the Dopamine Chain: There is a hard chemical reason why the "Three Things" rule works:

Dopamine isn't a reward for finishing; it's a fuel for continuing.

When you check off a task on a 47-item list, your brain doesn't give you a chemical high-five. It just looks at the 46 items remaining and says, "Great, only six more years of misery to go." You feel no satisfaction, only a temporary stay of execution. This is why you feel exhausted even when you've been productive all day—you're running on cortisol, not dopamine.

But when you finish one item on a three-item list, you are 33% finished with your entire day. That is a massive mathematical win. Your brain recognizes significant progress toward a goal and releases a hit of dopamine.

This dopamine hit acts as Rocket Fuel for Task Number Two. By shrinking the finish line, you actually make yourself move faster. You aren't doing less; you are finishing more. You're shifting from a defensive posture (trying not to fail the list) to an offensive posture (hunting the wins).

The hardest part of picking your "Three" is distinguishing between Urgent and Important. In corporate jobs (I worked as a sales manager of a company), everything feels urgent. Every notification is a fire.

But remember: urgency is often just someone else's lack of planning trying to become your emergency. If you spend your whole day putting out urgent fires, you are essentially letting other people edit your To-Do list. You are a passenger in your own career. The "Three Things" Rule forces you to be the Pilot. You have to look at the fire and say, "that can burn for another two hours. I have a Big Rock to move."

Here is where I (as a corporate snob) and the Specialist usually fail. You pick your three things, you sit down with your "Big Rock," and then... The Phone Rings. Or an "Urgent" email arrives with a subject line in all caps: "QUICK QUESTION – NEED BY COB."

In the old, chaotic way of working, you would immediately add this new emergency to your list. Your 3-item list would become a 4-item list, then a 5-item list, and by 3:00 PM, you're back in the Infinite Scroll of Despair. You've allowed the world to edit your priorities.

The "Three Things" Rule requires a Closed List Policy: Think of your daily list not as a notepad, but as a Bank Vault. Once the three things are chosen and the door is swung shut at 9:00 AM (or 2:00 PM if you're recovering from a Half-Day Trap), the vault is LOCKED. Nothing else gets in.

- The "Parking Lot" Protocol: If a new task arrives via email, text, or a shouting colleague, it goes into the Parking Lot (the notebook we established in Chapter 1). It does not get to interrupt the Big Rock.

- The "Boundary" Ritual: You have to treat your "Three Things" like VIP guests at an exclusive club. If their name isn't on the list, they aren't getting in until the party is over.

This feels mean. It feels unprofessional. You worry that people will think you're being unresponsive or "hard to work with." But remember, a person who replies to every email instantly but never actually closes a deal or moves the strategy forward is just a very polite, very responsive failure.

Being responsive is often just a fancy word for being consentingly distracted. The "Closed List" is how you protect the work that actually pays for your house and your sanity.

The "But What If I Finish Early?" Trap: This is the most common question I get from the Architects and the Firefighters. "If I only have three things on my list and I finish them by 3:00 PM, what do I do? Am I allowed to just... sit there?"

First, let's be honest: for most of us, finishing three actual priorities is a Herculean feat that usually takes the full day. But if you do hit that "Triple Crown" early, you have two choices, and only one of them is the method I use:

- The Overachiever's Trap: You immediately open the Parking Lot and pull in five more tasks. You keep working until your eyes bleed. Result: You burn through your remaining Decision Tokens, you end the day exhausted, and you teach your brain that "Winning" just results in "More Work." This is a fast track to the Sunday-night dread.

- The "Bonus Round" Strategy: You declare the day a Victory. You are now playing with "House Money." You can choose one more thing from the Parking Lot—something easy, something you want to do—or, heaven forbid, you can go home. You can go for a walk. You can be present with your family.

By stopping when the "Three" are done, you create a positive feedback loop. Your brain starts to realize that being productive has a finish line. It stops fighting you because it knows there is a reward (Rest) waiting at the end of the three checks.

The "Inertia" of the Fourth Task: Often, the momentum from the first three tasks is so strong that a fourth or fifth task feels effortless. That's fine. But the psychological difference is massive. Doing a fourth task because you choose to is an act of power; doing a fourteenth task because you have to is an act of a hostage.

The "Closed List" keeps you in the position of the Pilot. It ensures that even on your worst, most distracted Tuesday, you at least moved the three things that mattered most.

If you resonated at all with the Firefighter (Category 4), your natural instinct is to pick the three loudest things. You pick the client who is currently shouting, the email that has "URGENT" in red, and the bill that is three days overdue.

But as we established in Chapter 1, Loud is not the same as Important. To implement the "Three Things" Rule, you have to perform a Triage. In a hospital, the doctors don't treat the person who is screaming the loudest; they treat the person who is most at risk of dying. In your business or your legal practice, you have to treat the tasks that are most at risk of killing your momentum.

This is my suggestion: When you sit down to pick your three, ask yourself these three "High-Stakes" questions:

The "Leverage" Question: Which of these tasks, if finished, makes the rest of the week easier or even unnecessary? (This is usually your Big Rock).

The "Integrity" Question: Which of these tasks is a promise I've made to someone else that, if broken, damages my reputation or my business? (This is your first Pebble).

The "Anxiety" Question: Which of these tasks is currently eating up the most "Background RAM" in my brain? (This is the "Nagging" task—the one you've been avoiding for three days).

By picking one task that fits each of these, you create a "Balanced Portfolio" of productivity. You've moved the needle, you've kept your word, and you've cleared the mental fog.

The "Night Before" Hack: Preparing the Battlefield: Here is the secret weapon of the high-performance Architect (Category 1): The decision of "What to Do" should never happen on the day you are doing it.

When you wake up on Tuesday morning, your Decision Tokens are at their peak. If you spend those tokens "deciding" what to work on, you are wasting your most valuable currency on administrative overhead. It's like a General arriving at the battlefield and spending the first four hours of the fight deciding where to put the cannons.

The battle is already lost. The Night Before Ritual takes exactly five minutes: At 5:00 PM (or whenever you "Shutdown"), look at your Parking Lot.

Pick your Three Things for tomorrow. Write them down on a physical piece of paper. Not an app. Not a digital list. A physical, tactile piece of paper.

Put that paper on top of your keyboard or your laptop. When you sit down at 9:00 AM the next day, the "Pilot" has already given the orders. The "Soldier" just has to execute. You don't have to "think." You don't have to "prioritize." You just have to Start.

The "Shutdown" Ritual: Defining the Finish Line: The final piece of the "Three Things" puzzle is the Shutdown.

For most of us, the workday never really ends. We take it home in our pockets. We check emails during dinner. We think about the "Unfinished 44" while we're trying to sleep. This is why we feel like "Human Sloths" (Chapter 2)—we never actually recharge.

When you finish your three things and perform your "Night Before" prep for tomorrow, you are officially Done. You have "Closed the Vault." You have permission to stop being a "Worker" and start being a "Human."

By defining a clear finish line (the completion of the three things), you stop the "Shame-Spiral" from Chapter 1. You can look at yourself in the mirror and say, "I did exactly what I set out to do today. The rest can wait." That feeling of Completion is the most powerful antidepressant in the productivity world. It builds the "Self-Trust" required to show up again on Wednesday and do it all over again.

The Transition: From "What" to "How": Now that we have the Map (The Three Things Rule), we have a new problem. Even with only three things to do, the Astronaut in you is going to want to do them "Perfectly." You're going to want to spend four hours on Task Number One because you're afraid of it being "Average."

To survive the afternoon, we need to move from the System to the Standards. Welcome to Chapter 5: The "Good Enough" Manifesto. It's time to give yourself permission to be a "B-Minus" student so you can finally graduate from the "School of Doing Nothing."

Chapter 5: The "Good Enough" Manifesto (The Practical Science of Lowering the Bar)

If it is 2:00 PM and you are currently "polishing" an email, a report, or a proposal that was technically "finished" an hour ago, you are currently flushing your most valuable currency down the toilet. You aren't being "diligent." You are falling victim to one of the most expensive mathematical errors in the professional world: The Law of Diminishing Returns.

In economics, diminishing returns happen when you keep adding input (time, effort, caffeine) to a project, but the output (quality, results, money) starts to flatline. For the Astronaut (Category 3), this isn't just a graph in a textbook; it is the reason your Tuesdays evaporate.

The 80/20 of Effort: The "Magic Hour"

Most tasks follow a very specific trajectory. The first 20% of your effort usually produces 80% of the results:

- In the first twenty minutes of a "Vomit Draft" (I'll explain this further soon) you get the core idea down.

- In the first ten minutes of a sales call, the rapport is built.

- In the first hour of a legal brief, the winning argument is found.

This is the "Magic Hour." This is where you are a high-leverage, high-impact human being. If you stopped right there, you would have a "B-Minus" product that is entirely functional, clear, and ready to be used.

But the Perfectionist cannot stop there. Your ego looks at that 80% and sees the 20% that is missing. You see the slightly clunky sentence. You see the font that isn't quite "inspiring" enough. You see the three extra data points you could add if you just spent another two hours in the archives.

So, you keep working. You spend the next four hours trying to claw your way from 80% to 95%. The Math of the Last 10%. Here is the brutal reality of that "Polish" phase:

1. The Time Spike: That final 15% of quality will take you four times longer than the first 80% did.

2. The Invisible Gain: To you, the difference between an 80% version and a 95% version is "Life or Death." To your client, your boss, or your audience, the difference is invisible. They just want the answer. They just want the product. They don't

care about the three hours you spent choosing between "Arial" and "Helvetica."

3. The Opportunity Cost: This is the big one. Every hour you spend "polishing" a task that is already "Good Enough" is an hour you have stolen from your next "Big Rock."

When you spend all afternoon turning a "Good" document into a "Great" one, you aren't being a high-performer. You are being a thief. You are stealing the time you were supposed to spend on Task Number Two and Task Number Three. You end the day with one "Perfect" thing and two "Zero" things.

The math doesn't add up. Three "Good Enough" wins will always beat one "Perfect" win in the long run of a career.

The Law of Complexity: When "Perfect" Makes it Worse: There is a hidden danger in perfectionism that we rarely talk about: Over-engineering. When you spend too much time on a task, you often make it worse for the end-user. You add too many words. You add too many features. You add too much nuance. You turn a clear, "B-Minus" email that takes thirty seconds to read into a four-page "A-Plus" manifesto that your client will immediately mark as "Read Later" (which we all know means "Never").

By lowering the bar to "Good Enough," you are often doing the other person a favor. You are giving them the signal without the noise. You are giving them the "Vomit Draft" of the solution so they can get on with their day.

The Success Ceiling: Deciding When to Quit: To escape the Diminishing Returns Trap, you need to set a Success Ceiling before you even open your laptop.

Before you start Task Number One from your "Three Things" list, ask yourself: "What does 'Good Enough' look like for this?"

Does it mean the email is sent?

Does it mean the first 500 words are written?

Does it mean the invoice is filed?

Write that definition down. Once you hit that ceiling, you are legally required to stop. You are not allowed to "just give it one more pass." You have hit the point of diminishing returns. Any further effort is a waste of your Decision Tokens.

By setting a ceiling, you give your inner perfectionist a "Finish Line" that isn't "Perfection." You turn "Stopping" into a goal. You give yourself permission to walk away from a "B-Minus" because you know that "B-Minus" is the key to unlocking the rest of your day.

The Good Enough Manifesto isn't about being lazy. It's about being efficient. It's about realizing that in a world of people who are paralyzed by the "Last 10%," the person who consistently delivers "80% Quality" at "100% Speed" is the one who wins.

To actually hit that 80% mark before your afternoon energy drops off a cliff, you have to perform a neurological surgery on your workflow. You have to physically separate the part of your brain that assembles ideas from the part that judges them.

In a normal, stalled afternoon, these two parts of your brain are in a constant, low-level civil war. You type a sentence (Creation), you read it back, you hate the word "leverage," you delete it, you try "utilize," you realize "utilize" sounds like a middle-manager trying too hard, and you delete that too.

Ten minutes have passed. Your cursor is exactly where it started. You have expended the energy of a marathon runner while standing perfectly still. This is the "Edit-as-you-go" Trap, and it is the primary reason "Simple" tasks take four hours.

The Neurological Mismatch

Your brain is a dual-core processor, but it's not designed for parallel processing in this specific way.

- The Right Brain (The Generator): This is the messy, creative, "Vomit" phase. It's fast, it's intuitive, and it's deeply unconcerned with grammar or social standing.

- The Left Brain (The Editor): This is the precise, logical, "Clean-up" phase. It is obsessed with rules, standards, and how you appear to others.

When you try to edit while you create, you are forcing these two systems to fight for the same resources. It's like trying to sweep the floor while someone else is still throwing confetti in the air. The "Vomit Draft" is the process of letting the confetti fall until the floor is covered, and only then picking up the broom.

The "Zero-Backspace" Protocol: To master the Vomit Draft, you need to implement the Zero-Backspace Protocol. This is a high-speed, low-stakes sprint designed to bypass the Editor entirely.

1. Commit to the Mess: Tell yourself, "This version is supposed to be garbage. My only job is to fill the page." 2. The Physical Constraint: If you are a chronic deleter, try a "Blind Draft." Turn the brightness on your monitor all the way down so you can't see the words you're typing. Or, use a physical notebook and a pen—something you can't "delete."

2. The "Keep Moving" Rule: If you get stuck on a word, a fact, or a name, do not stop. Do not open a

new tab to "quickly check" a date. (We know where that leads—Chapter 2's Rabbit Hole).

3. The Placeholder Hack: Use brackets to mark the gaps. "[INSERT SMART QUOTE HERE]" or "[FIND THE EXACT REVENUE NUMBER LATER]". These are your "Structural Screws." They hold the draft together so you can keep building without stopping to polish the doorknobs.

The 15-Minute Sprint: The Vomit Draft shouldn't be a marathon. It should be a Sprint. Set a timer for fifteen minutes. Your goal isn't "quality"; it's volume. If you are writing an email, try to get the whole thing out in one go. If you are prepping a sales pitch, talk it out into a voice-memo app without stopping to correct your "umms" and "ahhs."

What you will find at the end of fifteen minutes is a disaster. It will be riddled with typos, half-formed thoughts, and probably a few accidental insults to the English language. But it will be a "Finished" Disaster.

Psychologically, the "Weight of the Task" has just vanished. You are no longer staring at the "Terror of the Blank Page." You are staring at a "Fix-it Job." And as we've established, the Perfectionist in you is a world-class fixer. By giving yourself a "Vomit Draft" to work with, you've handed your inner critic a shovel instead of a noose.

The "Done" Momentum: The beauty of the Vomit Draft is that it generates its own heat. When you see 300 words on a screen—even if they're 300 bad words—your brain registers a "Win." You have moved from 0 to 1.

In the Half-Day Trap, the move from 0 to 1 is the hardest move you will ever make. Once you are at 1, the "B-Minus" Revolution is already underway. You can spend ten minutes "tidying up" the vomit into a "Good Enough" 70% version, hit send, and move on to the next thing on your "Three Things" list.

You didn't wait for inspiration. You didn't wait for the "Perfect Word." You just made a mess and then put a bow on it.

Once you've vomited the draft and cleaned up the worst of the wreckage, you hit the most dangerous part of the afternoon: The Final 10%.

This is where the Perfectionist performs a "Silent Hijack." You've done the hard work. The email is 90% there. The report is accurate. The logic is sound. But then, a voice whispers: "Is 'robust' really the right word? Maybe 'comprehensive' is better. And should I double-check that case law from 2014 one more time? Just to be safe."

Stop. Right there. You are entering the Audit Phase, and if you aren't careful, this is where your 3:00 PM momentum goes to die.

The "Success Ceiling" vs. The "Success Floor"

Most people work toward a Success Floor—the bare minimum required not to get fired. Perfectionists, however, work toward an infinite sky. They have no ceiling. They will keep polishing until the clock runs out or they collapse.

To survive the Half-Day Trap, you must build a Success Ceiling before you start. You need to define exactly what "Done" looks like in objective, boring terms:

- The Email Ceiling: "The recipient has the answer they need and the tone is professional."

- The Report Ceiling: "The data is accurate and the three key recommendations are clear.

- The Sales Script Ceiling: "The value proposition is stated and there is a clear call to action."

Once you hit that ceiling, you are legally prohibited from continuing. Any further "polishing" is no longer "work"—it is Procrastination in a tuxedo. You are using "excellence" as a reason to avoid moving on to the next difficult thing on your "Three Things" list.

The Reputation Myth: Reliability > Brilliance

We tell ourselves that our reputation is built on our "brilliance." We think people value us because our work is flawless.

Here is the truth from the trenches of business and law: People value reliability far more than they value a 5%

increase in polish. * Your client doesn't want a "Perfect" contract next Thursday; they want a "Good" contract today so they can sign the deal.

Your team doesn't want a "Masterpiece" memo; they want a "Clear" memo so they can get to work.

When you hold onto a project to make it "perfect," you aren't being a high-achiever; you are being an unreliable bottleneck. You are the reason the project is stalled. By hitting "Send" on a "B-Minus" version that is 70% of your ideal, you are providing the most valuable service of all: Momentum.

The "Send" Ritual: The 3-Breath Rule

Hitting "Send" on imperfect work feels like jumping into a cold lake. Your ego screams that you've missed something. Your inner critic predicts a catastrophe.

To bypass this, use the 3-Breath Rule:

Breath One: Review the document one last time only for the "Success Ceiling" criteria.

Breath Two: Remind yourself that "Done is better than Perfect."

Breath Three: Hit the button.

Do not look at it again. Do not open your "Sent" folder to re-read it (the ultimate form of digital self-flagellation). The moment that document leaves your outbox, it is no longer your problem. You have "shipped the mess," and in doing so, you have freed up the mental RAM to tackle the next "Big Rock."

The Audit of the "I Could Have Done Better" Ghost: At the end of the day, the Perfectionist is often haunted by the "Ghost of Better." You sit on the couch and think about that one sentence you could have phrased better.

You need to perform a B-Minus Audit. Ask yourself: "Did the 'B-Minus' version achieve the goal?" In 99% of cases, the answer is yes. The client replied. The boss approved. The world didn't end. By proving to yourself—day after day—that "Good Enough" actually works, you start to dismantle the "Golden Cage" of perfectionism. You realize that "Perfect" was never the goal; Progress was.

If you have made it through the Vomit Draft and survived the B-Minus Audit, there is one final boss standing between you and a productive afternoon: The Quest for the Perfect Setup.

We have all done it. It's 2:45 PM. You have your "Three Things" list. You've given yourself permission to be average. But then, you look at your desk. There's a half-eaten sandwich wrapper. There are three pens that don't work. The lighting in the room feels "aggressive." Suddenly, you decide that you cannot possibly be brilliant until you have cleared the decks, lit a sandalwood candle, and found the perfect lo-fi beats playlist for "Focusing Like a CEO."

This is the Immaculate Vibes Fallacy. It is the belief that productivity is an ethereal spirit that only visits when the conditions are laboratory-grade perfect.

Procrastination in a Zen Coat

We need to call "getting ready to work" what it actually is: Productive Procrastination. When you spend thirty minutes tidying your office or "organizing" your digital folders before you start a task, you are telling your brain that the work is so fragile, so difficult, and so intimidating that it requires a pristine environment to survive. You are reinforcing the idea that you are a Fragile Producer.

A Fragile Producer can only work when the sun is out, the house is silent, and the coffee is the perfect temperature. If a neighbor starts mowing their lawn or a Slack notification pings, the Fragile Producer shatters. The afternoon is "ruined." The mission is scrubbed.

To escape the Half-Day Trap, you have to become a Robust Producer.

The "Working in the Rubble" Mindset

A Robust Producer doesn't need "Immaculate Vibes." They need a mission.

Think about a journalist writing a story on a deadline in a crowded newsroom, or a parent answering an urgent email while a toddler is using their leg as a climbing frame. They don't have the luxury of "vibes." They work in the rubble. They realize that the quality of the output has almost zero correlation with the aesthetic of the workspace.

- The 60-Second Rule: If it takes more than sixty seconds to "set up" your workspace, you are stalling.

- The "Messy Desk" Immunity: A stack of papers on your desk is not an obstacle; it's just scenery. Your brain is a supercomputer; it is perfectly capable of ignoring a coffee stain while drafting a contract.

- The Noise Adaptation: Stop waiting for silence. Silence is a myth in the modern world. Use white noise or simply accept the chaos as the "soundtrack of getting things done."

The "Rough Draft" Identity

The reason we crave "Immaculate Vibes" is that we want to feel like a "Professional." We think a professional has a clean desk and a clear mind.

But the real professionals—the ones who actually finish their Tuesdays—know that the "Professional" is the person who shows up when they feel like garbage, in a room that looks like a disaster, and produces a "B-Minus" result anyway.

Your identity should not be "The Person with the Best Results." That person is a hostage to their own expectations. Your identity should be "The Person who Always Delivers." When you shift your self-worth to Reliability and Momentum, the need for "perfect vibes" evaporates. You don't need a candle to be reliable. You don't need a $200 ergonomic chair to be a person who hits "Send."

The Shutdown: Embracing the "Good Enough" Day: As you close Chapter 5, I want you to look at your afternoon through a new lens.

If it's 4:00 PM and you've managed to produce a "Vomit Draft," audit it down to a "Good Enough" 70%, and hit "Send" while sitting in a messy room—you have won. You have defeated the Half-Day Trap. You didn't win because you were "Great." You won because you were brave enough to be average. You have reclaimed the second half of your day by lowering the stakes until the resistance had nothing to hold onto. You have dismantled the Golden Cage and replaced it with a Workman's Bench. Now that we've lowered the bar and mastered the ugly start, we have to deal with the one thing that can still pull us back into the abyss: The glowing rectangle in your pocket.

Welcome to Chapter 6: Distraction Jiu-Jitsu. It's time to turn your phone from your greatest enemy into your most reluctant sidekick.

Chapter 6: Distraction Jiu-Jitsu (Turning Your Phone from Enemy to Reluctant Sidekick)

Picture this: It's 2:37 p.m. on a perfectly ordinary Wednesday. You've just survived the Half-Day Trap (Chapter 2), forgiven yourself (again), chained three solid 5-Minute Rebellions (Chapter 3), picked your Three Things like a responsible adult (Chapter 4), and even managed to vomit-draft something vaguely useful without polishing it into oblivion (Chapter 5). You're feeling… almost smug.

You lean back in your chair, stretch your arms, take a triumphant sip of what was once hot coffee but is now a lukewarm beverage of questionable origin, and think: "Look at me. I'm actually getting things done. I might even finish before the sun sets on this godforsaken day."

And then your phone buzzes. Not a real buzz. Not an emergency. Just that tiny, innocent haptic tickle that says: "Someone liked your story from three days ago when you tried to look cool holding a flat white." You glance at it. You tell yourself: "I'll just check who it was. One second." You unlock the screen.

Forty-seven minutes later you know:

The full plot of a Netflix show you've never watched,
That your high-school classmate's cousin just got engaged
in Santorini,
The correct way to pronounce "gif" (you still think you're
right),
And that there's a limited-time 20% off deal on noise-
cancelling headphones you don't need but suddenly
desperately want.

Your Three Things are still sitting there, untouched
since the last rebellion ended. The smug feeling is gone. In
its place is the familiar, cold knot of "I did it again."

Welcome to my life. Welcome to most of our lives. My
phone isn't a tool anymore. It's a needy ex who keeps
texting at 2 a.m. with memes, guilt trips, and the occasional
"u up?" from an algorithm that knows exactly how weak
my dopamine receptors are. I've had full-blown arguments
with it in my head. I've hidden it in drawers, turned it face-
down, put it on Do Not Disturb, only to fish it out thirty
seconds later because "what if it's important this time?"
Spoiler: It never is.

I once tried the nuclear option. I deleted Instagram,
Twitter, TikTok, YouTube, even the news app—everything

except phone calls, texts, and my banking app. I lasted forty-seven glorious minutes. Then I told myself I just needed to "check the weather." Forty-seven minutes after that I was deep in a thread debating whether cats dream in color, and somehow I'd re-downloaded three apps "just in case."

That's when I realized the truth: Going cold turkey doesn't work for people like us. We're not built for monastic silence. We're built for chaos, novelty, and the occasional dopamine hit that feels like love for three seconds. Trying to banish the phone completely is like trying to banish gravity because you keep falling over. It's not going anywhere. And honestly? It's useful. It has calendars, timers, voice notes, maps, calculators, and—on rare occasions—actual human connection.

So, the goal isn't to kill the phone. The goal is to stop letting it kill your afternoons.

This chapter isn't about becoming one of those terrifying digital-minimalist monks who only check email once a week on a flip phone they keep in a Faraday pouch. (If that's you, respect. But also... how do you order Uber Eats?)

This is about jiu-jitsu. Using the phone's own momentum against it. Turning it from the enemy that drags you into rabbit holes to a reluctant, slightly sulky sidekick that occasionally does what you ask.

We're not aiming for perfection here. We're aiming for "I now lose only twenty minutes instead of two hours." That's progress. That's a win. And if you slip and lose the full two hours again? Forgive yourself. Reset the timer. Start again.

Because the second half of the day is still yours. Even if your phone is trying very hard to convince you otherwise.

Ready to put a leash on the little glowing rectangle? Well, we need to first accept that they're winning.

Why Phones Are So Damn Good at Winning

Let's not pretend we're above it. We all know the phone is winning. We just pretend we're letting it win "strategically" while we secretly hope it'll get bored and leave us alone.

The truth is simpler and more embarrassing: phones are engineered to be better at this game than we are. They're not accidents. They're slot machines that fit in your pocket, built by people who studied psychology the way a casino studies probability.

Remember the variable reward schedule we touched on in Chapter 2? That's the polite name for it. The rude name is "how they keep you pulling the lever like a trained rat."

Every pull (refresh, scroll, notification) might give you nothing… or it might give you the perfect hit. Your brain doesn't know which it'll be. That uncertainty is the drug. It's the same mechanism that keeps people at poker machines until the kids' college fund is gone. Except instead of quarters, they're using your attention, your afternoon, and increasingly your sense of self-worth.

Then there's the social proof layer. Every heart, comment, share, view count is a tiny "you matter" signal from the tribe. Our ancient wiring still cares desperately about belonging. A thousand years ago, being liked by the group meant you didn't get left behind when the tribe moved camp. Today it means someone double-tapped your avocado toast. Same circuitry, different stakes.

And FOMO? Fear Of Missing Out is just the modern rebrand of "if I don't check now I'll be the last to know and the tribe will laugh at me." The algorithm knows this. It shows you what your friends are doing, what strangers are achieving, what everyone else seems to have figured out—right when you're feeling a little behind. It's not random. It's personal.

Add infinite scroll (no natural stopping point), autoplay videos (no need to decide to keep watching), and push notifications (interrupting you before you even realize you're bored), and you have a machine that is better at hijacking your attention than almost anything in human history.

Your prefrontal cortex—the adult in the room who's supposed to say "put it down and finish the report"—is fighting a limbic system that thinks it's still living in a world where novelty = survival and social rejection = death. The limbic system is winning because it's faster, louder, and has been optimized by several billion dollars of A/B testing.

Here's the part that usually gets left out of the "phones are evil" lectures: This doesn't make you weak. It makes you normal. Very, very normal.

The people who seem to have perfect phone discipline either: a) have a different dopamine baseline (lucky them), b) have outsourced the battle to extreme systems (monk mode, flip phones, app blockers that require a blood oath to disable), or c) are lying on Instagram about how productive they are.

Most of us are in the middle: we want to get stuff done, we like some parts of the phone (music, timers, quick photos of funny signs), but we hate how easily it turns a productive afternoon into a highlight-reel binge.

The good news? Understanding the mechanics is half the rebellion. Once you see the slot machine for what it is, you stop feeling morally defective every time you lose forty minutes. You start seeing it as a game you can play better—not by refusing to play, but by changing the rules so the house doesn't always win.

We're not going to out-willpower the algorithm. That's a mug's game. We're going to out-smart it. A little bit. One tiny jiu-jitsu move at a time.

Because if we can turn even 20% of those lost hours into actual progress, that's not just a productivity win. That's stealing your life back from a machine that was never designed to give it back.

So, let's stop feeling ashamed of losing to the phone. Let's start treating it like the chaotic, brilliant, slightly sociopathic sidekick it actually is. We need to stop seeing the phone as the Enemy and start seeing it as a Chaotic Puppy.

A puppy isn't "evil." It's just biologically programmed to chase every squirrel, sniff every fire hydrant, and trip you up with its own leash because it saw a discarded chip packet. If you hit the puppy or lock it in a dark room forever, you aren't "training" it; you're just creating a traumatized animal that will eventually bite you.

The goal of Distraction Jiu-Jitsu is to train the puppy. We want to move from being dragged down the street by the algorithm to being the one holding the leash.

Control the Leash, Not the Dog: Training the puppy starts with a core mantra: "I don't need to be perfect; I just need to be the boss."

When you have a "relapse" and find yourself forty minutes deep into a Wikipedia rabbit hole about the Great Emu War, the old you would have spiraled into shame. The "Sidekick" version of you looks at the phone and says, "Okay, the puppy got loose. It happens. Let's get back on the path."

I tried going phone-free for a day once. I felt like a pioneer. I felt enlightened. I lasted exactly 71 minutes (I actually don't know) before I decided I "just needed to check the weather" to see if I should hang the washing out. One hour later, I wasn't hanging washing; I was looking up the capital of Mongolia (it's Ulaanbaatar, by the way) and checking if they have good coffee there.

The phone-free life is a myth for people who have actual jobs and lives. Instead, we want the Reluctant Sidekick. We want the phone to sit in the corner, slightly sulky because it's not allowed to beep at us, waiting until we decide it's time to play.

We are moving from a Push relationship (the phone tells you what to do) to a Pull relationship (you use the phone for a specific purpose, then put it back).

To do that, we need to get physical. We need the actual jiu-jitsu moves that turn a $1,500 distraction machine into a boring, functional tool.

Move 1: The Notification Curfew (Selective Muting)

The first and most brutal jiu-jitsu move is to strip the phone of its power to interrupt. We have been conditioned to treat every vibration in our pocket like a heart monitor flatlining, but let's be real: 99% of your notifications are digital confetti. They are "likes" from people you haven't seen since 2012 and "breaking news" about a celebrity's skincare routine.

You need to implement a notification curfew. This isn't about "Do Not Disturb"—which we all know is a lie because we just check the screen anyway—it's about selective muting.

Go into your settings and perform a digital massacre. Turn off every single notification except for 1–3 "VIPs." These are the only people allowed to bypass the moat: your spouse, your business partner, or that one specific client who actually pays on time. Everything else—Slack, Instagram, News, even your "Step Tracker" that keeps shaming you for sitting down—gets muted; where you check things on *your* terms. My phone is now quieter than my inner critic, and honestly, the silence is the most productive thing I've ever "heard."

Move 2: The Analog Parking Lot (The Brain's "Save" Button)

We've touched on the "Shiny Object" syndrome in Chapter 1, but when you're in the middle of a work block, your brain will betray you with essential intrusive thoughts.

Instead, use the Analog Leash Parking Lot method. Keep a physical notebook or a single piece of paper next to your laptop. When a "Shiny Thought" pops up, write it down immediately. Tell your brain: *"I've saved this. We aren't going to forget it."* Then, close the book. Psychologically, writing it down satisfies the "Zeigarnik Effect" mentioned earlier (remember?).

Move 3: Phone Jail and Temptation Bundling

If you can't stop yourself from reaching for the phone, you have to make the reach physically impossible. This is Phone Jail. During your 5-Minute Rebellions or your "Three Things" blocks, the phone does not stay on the desk. It goes in another room. It goes in a drawer. It goes anywhere that requires you to physically stand up and walk to get it.

That five-second walk is the "Jiu-Jitsu" move. It gives your adult brain a chance to wake up and ask, *"Is this Instagram scroll really worth the walk of shame to the kitchen?"* Usually, the answer is no.

To make the "boring" work more palatable, pair it with Temptation Bundling. I have a rule: I am only allowed to listen to my favorite true-crime podcasts or that one specific "guilty pleasure" playlist while I am doing the administrative tasks I hate—like answering emails or filing expenses. I am literally bribing myself with entertainment to stay in the chair. The phone becomes the "Record Player" in the corner, not the distraction in my hand.

Move 4: Grayscale Mode (The 2005 Nokia Hack)

Your phone is designed to look like a bowl of Skittles. The red notification bubbles and the vibrant app icons are specifically tuned to trigger your primitive "foraging" brain. We hunt for red fruit; we hunt for red notifications.

Turn on Grayscale Mode. (It's usually tucked away in Accessibility settings). Instantly, your $1,500 masterpiece of technology looks like a 2005 Nokia. It's flat. It's gray. It's depressing. And I bet you didn't even know this feature existed.

Suddenly, Instagram isn't seductive. TikTok looks like a dusty documentary from the 1950s. Your brain takes one look at the gray screen and says, *"Well, this is boring. I might as well go back to work."* You haven't used willpower; you've just removed the visual sugar.

Move 5: The One-Tab Oath (Browser Hygiene)

Your browser is likely a hoarder's living room right now. You have 27 tabs open, each one a tiny portal to a different distraction. This is a massive drain on your mental RAM.

Implement the One-Tab Oath. When you are working on a task, you are allowed **one** tab. If you need a second one for research, you open it, get the info, and *close it immediately.*

At the end of every work session—before you get up to stretch or grab a coffee—you perform the Tab Massacre. You close everything. You reset the board. Starting the next task with a clean browser is the digital equivalent of a deep breath. It's minimalist chic, by force.

Move 6: The Sidekick Check-In

Finally, stop trying to go "Phone-Free" for eight hours. You'll fail, feel like a loser, and binge for three hours to compensate.

Instead, use the Sidekick Check-In. Every 60 to 90 minutes—*after* you've finished one of your Three Things—give yourself a 2-minute "Phone Reward." Set a timer. Scroll, check the likes, see who got engaged in Santorini. When the timer pings, the sidekick goes back in the drawer. By scheduling the "distraction," you take the power away from the "Urge." You aren't depriving yourself; you're just deferring the reward until the work is done.

But here is the truth that the "hustle culture" gurus won't tell you: **You cannot maintain this level of Jiu-Jitsu forever.**

There will be a Tuesday where the puppy breaks the leash. There will be an afternoon where the "Half-Day Trap" feels like quicksand, and no amount of 5-Minute Rebellions can pull you out. There will be days where you do everything right, and you still feel like a "Category 4 Firefighter" trying to put out a forest fire with a water pistol.

In the old world—the world of the Golden Cage— those days were considered "failures." They were the days you'd use to prove to yourself that you're lazy, disorganized, and destined to be late to your own life.

But in this world, those aren't failures. They are data.

If you've spent the last six chapters learning how to fight for your afternoon, you need to spend the next one learning how to stop fighting and start recovering. Because the secret to a productive Tuesday isn't just what you do at 2:00 p.m.; it's how you handled the "crash" on Monday night.

It's time to talk about the part of productivity that makes the high-achievers twitch: Strategic Laziness. Let's head into **Part 3: Keeping the Momentum Without Face-Planting**. We're going to learn why Netflix only counts as rest if you stop feeling guilty about it, and why your "off" switch is just as important as your "on" switch. Turn the page. It's time to go home.

PART 3: KEEPING THE MOMENTUM WITHOUT FACE-PLANTING

Chapter 7: The Recovery Day: Rest Isn't Laziness, It's Strategic Recharging (Netflix Counts If You Don't Feel Guilty About It)

Now, sometimes after you successfully win back the day or finish those tasks you will be absolutely done. Tapped out even. You aren't just tired; you are cognitively bankrupt. You stand in front of the open refrigerator, staring at a carton of eggs and a jar of pickles as if they are ancient hieroglyphics you've been tasked to translate. Your spouse asks what you want for dinner, and the mere act of choosing between "Thai" or "Pizza" feels like a personal assault. Your "Decision Tokens" (Chapter 2) aren't just low; the treasury is empty. The vault is bare. So, you do what most high-achievers do: you "rest."

You collapse onto the couch, still wearing your work socks, and you pull out your phone. You spend the next two hours scrolling through LinkedIn to see what your competitors are doing, or checking Slack "just to make sure nothing exploded" while a Netflix documentary about a serial killer plays in the background.

Two hours later, you go to bed. But you don't sleep. Your brain is still humming at the frequency of a downed power line. You're thinking about that email you sent at 4:30 p.m. You're wondering if you phrased that one clause correctly. You wake up on Friday morning feeling like you've been hit by a truck—even though you "rested" all evening.

The Lie of "Productive Rest": Here is the confession: I spent a decade thinking that rest was a moral failing. I thought that if I wasn't "producing," I was rotting. I treated my brain like a rented mule—something to be whipped until it reached the destination, regardless of how much it was limping.

When I finally did sit down to relax, I practiced what I now call Dirty Rest. Dirty Rest is when you are physically still, but mentally "red-lining." It's watching a movie while your brain is secretly drafting tomorrow's "Three Things" list. It's "relaxing" at the beach while your eyes are glued to your inbox. It's the constant, low-grade hum of guilt that tells you that every minute you aren't being "useful" is a minute you're falling behind.

In the Golden Cage of perfectionism (Chapter 5), we believe that we have to earn the right to turn the engine off. We think of rest as the "prize" for a finished to-do list. But since the to-do list is a living, breathing monster that never actually dies, we never truly rest. We just face-plant.

This chapter is your formal invitation to stop earning your rest and start scheduling it as a high-performance tactic. If Chapter 6 was about putting a leash on the chaotic puppy of distraction, Chapter 7 is about letting the puppy sleep so it doesn't bite your hand off tomorrow morning.

We are going to move from "Dirty Rest" to Strategic Recovery.

The "Red-Line" Reality: In the world of high-performance engines, there is a "Red-Line"—the maximum speed at which the engine can operate without blowing itself apart. You can push into the red for a few seconds during a drag race, but if you try to drive from Brisbane to Cairns with the needle pinned in the red, you're going to end up on the side of the Bruce Highway with smoke pouring out of the bonnet.

Most of us spend our afternoons trying to "red-line" our decision-making.

As a professional, you aren't just "working." you are performing high-level cognitive labour. Every time you interpret a clause, every time you pivot a sales strategy, and every time you use "Distraction Jiu-Jitsu" to ignore a notification, you are burning fuel. This fuel isn't just calories; it's a specific neurochemical resource.

Decision Fatigue vs. Physical Fatigue:

The reason the "Face-Plant" (Section 1) feels so confusing is that you don't feel "tired" in your body. Your legs work fine. You could go for a jog. But your brain feels like it's been stuffed with cotton wool.

This is Decision Fatigue. The human brain accounts for about 2% of your body weight but consumes 20% of your energy. By 3:00 p.m., if you've been fighting the "Half-Day Trap," your brain has physically depleted its glucose stores in the Prefrontal Cortex. When that happens, the "Adult in the Room" goes on strike.

This is why, at 7:00 p.m., you can't decide between Thai or Pizza. It's not that you're "lazy"; it's that the part of your brain responsible for weighing options has literally run out of gas. If you try to force it to keep working, you aren't being "disciplined"—you are being a bad mechanic.

The Stress-Recovery-Adaptation Model: To fix this, we need to borrow a concept from sports science: The SRA Curve.

In weightlifting, you don't get stronger *while* you are lifting the barbell. Lifting the barbell actually tears your muscle fibers. You are technically "weaker" the moment you leave the gym. You get stronger during the recovery phase—when you are eating, sleeping, and *not* lifting things.

Your productivity works the exact same way.

Stress: The 5-Minute Rebellions, the Three Things, the intense legal drafting.

Recovery: The "Off-Switch." The strategic silence. The actual rest.

Adaptation: This is where your brain "defragments" the day's info, stores it in long-term memory, and resets your "Decision Tokens" for tomorrow.

If you skip the Recovery, you never reach the Adaptation. You just stay in the "Dip." You show up on Friday morning with the same depleted treasury you had on Thursday night.

The "Terminally Wired" Trap:

The problem for people like us—the "Terminally Disorganized" but "High-Achieving" hybrids—is that our brains are "Sticky." We find it very hard to disengage the gears. We think that by worrying about work at 9:00 p.m., we are somehow "getting a head start" on tomorrow.

We aren't. We are just idling the engine in the garage. We're burning fuel without moving an inch.

To win the week, you have to accept a radical, uncomfortable truth: **The quality of your Wednesday depends entirely on how well you "wasted" your Tuesday night.**

If you want to be a "Robust Producer" (Chapter 5), you have to become a "Professional Rester." You have to learn the difference between "collapsing" and "recovering." To become a "Professional Rester," you have to audit how you actually spend your downtime. Most of us are addicted to a middle-ground state that provides zero recovery while still burning mental RAM. This is the difference between filling your tank with high-octane fuel and filling it with sugar water.

The "Clean Rest" Protocol:

Clean Rest, on the other hand, is a deliberate, guilt-free shutdown. It is the act of completely severing the connection between your identity and your output for a specific window of time.

When you practice Clean Rest, your brain enters Default Mode Processing. This is when the "Defragmenter" starts running. It's the mental equivalent of cleaning up a messy workshop at the end of the day. Your brain sorts through the "confetti" of the afternoon, files the important stuff, and deletes the trash.

But here's the catch: The Defragmenter can only run when you stop giving it new data to process. If you are "resting" by scrolling social media, you are feeding the machine more data. The workshop never gets cleaned.

The "Sticky Brain" Problem:

The reason we struggle with Clean Rest is that our brains are "sticky." We find it physically uncomfortable to let go of the day's problems. We tell ourselves that by "mulling it over" while we eat dinner, we are being responsible. In reality, you are just overheating the engine.

Think of your brain like a high-performance lightbulb. If you leave it on 24/7, the filament will eventually burn out. It doesn't matter how "important" the light is; physics doesn't care about your deadlines. To keep the bulb working tomorrow, you have to flip the switch tonight.

The Rebrand: Rest as a Weapon

To win this movement, you have to stop seeing rest as "the absence of work." You have to start seeing it as The Foundation of Work.

You don't rest because you're finished; you rest so that you *can* finish tomorrow. Clean rest isn't a luxury; it's a tactical requirement. If you aren't scheduling "Off-Time" where the phone is in another room and the brain is "offline," you aren't being a high-performer—you're just a machine waiting to break.

To bridge the gap between "Dirty Rest" and "Clean Rest," you need a set of physical cues. Because your brain is a "sticky" machine, you can't just tell it to stop thinking about work; you have to prove to it that the workday is over. Similar to our phone devices, we have jiu-jitsu moves (or maybe kung fu moves?) to implement and action.

Here are the four moves for high-performance recovery.

Move 1: The Shutdown Ritual

The biggest mistake we make is "bleeding" out of our workspace. We finish a task, close the laptop lid halfway, and walk into the kitchen while still mentally debating a sentence. Your brain doesn't know you've left the office because your environment hasn't changed.

You need a Shutdown Ritual. It takes five minutes, but it saves five hours of evening anxiety.

The Final Brain Dump: Write down the "Three Things" for tomorrow. This "parks" the worries so they don't have to loop in your head all night.

The Physical Clear: Close every tab. Straighten your pens. Wipe the desk.

The Verbal Cue: Say it out loud. "The day is done." It sounds cheesy, but it's a powerful neurological signal.

Move 2: The "Guilt-Free Netflix" Protocol

Netflix is a fantastic recovery tool, but only if you use it correctly. Most people use it as "background noise" while they scroll on their phones. This is the definition of Dirty Rest.

To turn TV into Clean Rest, follow the Selection Rule: Decide exactly what you are going to watch before you sit down. Don't browse for forty minutes. Choose one movie or two episodes of a show. Put the phone in another room. Watch the screen with 100% of your attention. By immersing yourself in a story, you are forcing your brain to stop processing your own life and start processing someone else's. That is where the recharging happens.

Move 3: The "Nature Pill"

There is a concept in psychology called Attention Restoration Theory (ART). It suggests that urban environments—with their traffic, sirens, and glowing screens—exhaust our "Directed Attention" (the focus we use for work).

Nature, however, provides "Soft Fascination." Looking at a tree, the ocean, or even just the clouds doesn't require "Directed Attention." It allows your brain to idle.

The Move: Spend 15 minutes outside without a podcast, without a phone, and without a goal. Just look at something that isn't a rectangle. This is the fastest way to reset your parasympathetic nervous system and move from "Fight or Flight" back into "Rest and Digest."

Move 4: The Digital Sabbath (Light Version)

If you want to truly defragment the hard drive, you need a period of Total Disconnection. For the terminally disorganized, a full 24-hour "Digital Sabbath" feels like a prison sentence.

Start with the Light Version: Pick a 4-hour block on Sunday. Put the "Chaotic Puppy" (your phone) in a drawer. Turn off the computer. During these four hours, you are "off the grid." Go for a walk, read a physical book, or have a conversation where nobody checks a notification.

The first hour will feel itchy. Your brain will scream for a dopamine hit. But by the third hour, something magical happens: your "Decision Tokens" start to grow back. You'll find yourself having creative ideas again—not because you're trying, but because you finally gave your brain enough space to breathe.

The Zero-Output Assignment

Now, it's time to put the theory into practice. This isn't a "to-do" item; it is a "to-don't" item. To close out this chapter and prepare for the final stretch of the book, you are going to perform one Strategic Recovery move tonight.

The Challenge: The 30-Minute "Ghost" Window

Tonight, between finishing your work and going to sleep, you are going to create a 30-minute window where you are a "ghost" to the digital world.

The Drop: Put your phone in a drawer, a different room, or—if you're feeling particularly rebellious—the glove box of your car.

The Rule: You are legally prohibited from being "useful." You cannot "quickly check" a calendar, you cannot "just tidy up" the kitchen, and you certainly cannot listen to an educational podcast.

The Activity: You must do something that provides Soft Fascination. Sit on the porch and look at the streetlights. Read five pages of a fiction book. Listen to one album from start to finish without doing anything else.

What to Expect: For the first ten minutes, you will feel like you are failing. Your brain will offer you a thousand "important" things you should be doing instead. It will try to convince you that this 30-minute break is the reason you aren't more successful.

Ignore it. That's just the "Sticky Brain" trying to stay in the Red-Line.

By minute twenty, the itch will start to fade. By minute thirty, you will feel a strange, cool clarity. This is your Decision Tokens being minted. This is the "Adaptation" phase of the SRA curve finally kicking in.

The Mantra. Repeat after me: "My value is not defined by my 8:00 p.m. output. My 8:00 a.m. performance is defined by my 8:00 p.m. recovery."

You aren't being lazy. You're being a professional.

The Transition: From Being to Doing.

Now that we've learned how to turn the engine off without crashing, we have a new problem: Sustainability. It's one thing to have a "Heroic Tuesday" where you use every jiu-jitsu move in the book. It's another thing to do it again on Wednesday, Thursday, and Friday without exhausting your willpower.

In the next chapter, we're going to stop relying on "tactics" and start relying on Architecture. We're going to look at Habit Stacking for the Terminally Disorganised. We're going to learn how to "piggyback" your new productivity onto the things you already do—like brushing your teeth or making coffee—so that being productive becomes as automatic as breathing.

Turn the page. Let's make this easy.

Chapter 8: Habit Stacking for the Terminally Disorganized (Link New Stuff to Things You Already Do… Like Breathing)

The "I'll Do It Monday" Mirage

We have all been there. It is Sunday night, and you are feeling a surge of "New Me" energy. You've decided that starting tomorrow, you will wake up at 5:00 a.m., drink a liter of lemon water, meditate for twenty minutes, journal your intentions, and crush your "Three Things" before the sun even thinks about rising. By Monday at 2:00 p.m., you are face-down in a bag of salt-and-vinegar chips, your journal is being used as a coaster, and you haven't seen a drop of water that wasn't inside a coffee bean.

The reason your "New Life" resolutions fail isn't that you lack willpower. It's that you are trying to build a skyscraper on a foundation of sand. You are trying to install "High-Performance Software" into a brain that is still running on "Terminally Disorganized" hardware.

If you want your productivity to stick, you have to stop relying on Motivation (which is a fickle friend who disappears the moment you're tired) and start relying on Architecture. Welcome to Habit Stacking.

The "Piggyback" Principle:

If you've ever tried to start a new habit—like "I'm going to meditate for twenty minutes every morning"—and failed by Wednesday, it's probably because you were trying to build a brand-new bridge in the middle of a swamp. There was nothing to anchor it to.

Your brain is a remarkably efficient (read: lazy) machine. It loves "Neural Pathways." These are the physical grooves in your brain created by repetition. You have a "Superhighway" for brushing your teeth. You have a "Deep Trench" for putting on your seatbelt. You don't have to think about these things because the neurons involved have fired together so many times they've basically fused into an autopilot setting.

The Anchor and the Attachment

The Piggyback Principle—or Habit Stacking—is about finding one of those existing "Superhighways" and hitching your new, fragile habit to it. You aren't building a new road; you're just adding a passenger to a car that's already driving in that direction.

In this relationship, your old habit is the Anchor. It's the thing that is 100% going to happen regardless of your willpower. Your new habit is the Attachment.

Why "Willpower" is the Wrong Tool

When you say, *"I'll just remember to do my Three Things list,"* you are relying on your Directed Attention. This is a high-energy, expensive resource that runs out the moment you get a stressful email or a bad night's sleep.

When you say, *"After I turn on the kettle, I will write my Three Things,"* you are outsourcing the "remembering" to the kettle. The kettle becomes your external hard drive. The moment you hear that click or see the steam, your brain triggers the next step automatically.

The Physics of the Stack

For a "Terminally Disorganized" brain, the stack works best when it follows the laws of physics:

1. Proximity: The new habit should happen in the same physical space as the old one. If you want to stack "Journaling" onto "Coffee," put the journal on top of the coffee machine.
2. Immediate Sequence: There should be zero "Gap Time" between the anchor and the attachment. If you wait ten minutes, the "Neural Spark" dies, and you're back to relying on willpower.

By tethering your productivity to your existing biological and domestic rhythms—like coffee, lunch, or even the act of sitting in your office chair—you stop fighting your nature. You start using the "Deep Trenches" of your brain to pull you toward the person you want to be.

This is where the "Golden Cage" of perfectionism (Chapter 5) usually swoops in and ruins everything. Your perfectionist brain hears "Habit Stacking" and immediately wants to build a triple-decker, high-performance sandwich.

It thinks: "After I pour my first coffee, I will write 2,000 words, meditate for twenty minutes, and do fifty push-ups."

That isn't a habit stack; that's a suicide mission for your willpower. By Tuesday morning, the sight of the coffee machine will trigger a wave of performance anxiety so strong you'll consider switching to tea just to avoid the "required" productivity.

The "Two-Minute Entry" Rule

If you want a habit to stick in a "Terminally Disorganized" brain, the Attachment must be so small that it feels pathetic to say no to it. It should be so easy that you could do it even if you had a migraine, your car wouldn't start, and the QLD humidity was at 99%.

The rule is simple: The start of the habit must take less than two minutes.

Don't stack: "After I sit at my desk, I'll finish the report."

Do stack: "After I sit at my desk, I'll open the file and write one sentence."

The Physics of the "Pathetic" Win

Why does this work? Because for people like us, the hardest part isn't the work; it's the Transition into the work. We are objects at rest that really, really want to stay at rest (usually on the couch).

Once you've opened the file and written one sentence, the "Friction" of starting is gone. You've already "won" the stack. You've satisfied the neurological requirement. Usually, once you've written one sentence, you'll write ten more. But even if you don't—even if you just write that one sentence and walk away—you have kept the "Superhighway" in your brain open.

Keeping the "Path" Clear

A habit is like a path through a forest. If you walk it every day, even just for two minutes, the grass stays down. If you skip a week because the "task" felt too big, the weeds grow back, and suddenly "starting again" feels like a massive machete-swinging expedition.

We aren't aiming for a "Heroic Stack." We are aiming for a Non-Negotiable Stack.

Your brain needs to believe that the Attachment is just as inevitable as the Anchor. Coffee leads to opening the notebook. Brushing teeth leads to one deep breath. Putting on your shoes leads to checking your "Three Things."

If it's too small to fail, you'll actually do it. And doing something small 100% of the time beats doing something big 10% of the time every single day of the week.

Some Tools For You:

Another perspective for those who start their day late is this; your biggest enemies aren't the big tasks; they are the Transitions. These are the "liminal spaces" between one part of your life and the next.

The moment you finish your sandwich at lunch. The moment you pull the car into the driveway after the school run or a grocery trip. The moment you close a Zoom call. These are the Danger Zones.

In these gaps, your brain is "un-tethered." It's looking for a direction, and if you don't give it one, it will default to the path of least resistance: the phone, the fridge, or the "just five minutes" on the couch that turns into a two-hour coma.

We are going to use Habit Stacking to build "bridges" across these gaps.

The "Late Starter" Stack Pack

Here are four specific stacks designed for the terminally disorganized brain. Pick one to start with tomorrow.

The Kettle/Coffee Stack (The Morning Anchor)

The Anchor: Turning on the kettle or starting the coffee machine.

The Attachment: Scribbling your "Three Things" (Chapter 4) on a Post-it note.

Why it works: You're standing there anyway. You can't leave until the water boils. Instead of checking emails while you wait, you "prime" your brain for the win.

The "Office Doorway" Stack (The Boundary Anchor)

The Anchor: Crossing the threshold into your workspace (or sitting in your "Work Chair").

The Attachment: Putting your phone into "Phone Jail" (the drawer or the shelf).

Why it works: You are linking a physical location to a state of focus. Your brain starts to learn: When we sit here, the glowing rectangle disappears.

The Lunch Plate Stack (The Afternoon Bridge)

The Anchor: Putting your lunch plate in the dishwasher (or the sink).

The Attachment: Setting a timer for one 5-Minute Rebellion (Chapter 3).

Why it works: The "Afternoon Slump" usually starts right after lunch. By stacking a 5-minute win onto the act of cleaning up, you prevent the slump before it even begins. You're already standing up—keep the momentum going.

The "Key Hook" Stack (The End-of-Day Anchor)

The Anchor: Hanging up your car keys or closing your laptop lid for the day.

The Attachment: One 30-second "Final Brain Dump" in your Analog Parking Lot.

Why it works: This is the beginning of your Clean Rest (Chapter 7). By dumping the "leftover" thoughts the moment you finish, you prevent them from "bleeding" into your evening.

The Secret Sauce: "Trigger Sensitivity"

The reason these work is that they rely on External Triggers. You don't have to remember to do them; the kettle, the dishwasher, and the car keys remind you.

If you find yourself failing a stack, it's usually because the trigger isn't obvious enough. If that happens, make the trigger louder. Put the Post-it notes on the kettle. Put the "Phone Jail" box on your keyboard.

We are moving from a life of "trying to remember" to a life of "can't forget." A major key to that is the environment too!

Habit stacking is the engine, but your environment is the fuel. If you want to stack journaling onto morning coffee, but your journal is buried under a stack of unpaid bills in the spare room, the stack will fail every single time.

For the terminally disorganized, friction is the ultimate habit-killer. If it takes more than five seconds to find the tool you need for your "Attachment," your brain will use that gap to convince you that checking Instagram is a better use of your time. To make your stacks stick, you have to Prime the Space.

The "Path of Least Resistance"

Think of your habits like water flowing down a hill. Water doesn't "choose" where to go; it simply follows the path of least resistance. If you want a habit to happen, you have to dig the trench for it in advance.

The Coffee Stack: Don't just plan to write your Three Things while the kettle boils. Put the Post-it notes and a working pen *on top of the coffee machine* the night before.

The Office Doorway Stack: Place your "Phone Jail" box (the Reluctant Sidekick's home) directly in the center of your desk so you have to physically move it to sit down.

The 5-Minute Rebellion Stack: If your rebellion involves drafting a document, leave that document open as the only tab on your laptop before you go to lunch.

Visual Cues vs. Invisible Intentions

Your brain is a visual processor. If you can't see the trigger, the habit doesn't exist. This is why "out of sight, out of mind" is a literal biological reality for people with ADHD or chaotic schedules.

We need to move from Intentions (which are invisible) to Visual Cues (which are unavoidable).

If you want to do a "Final Brain Dump" when you hang up your keys, hang the notebook *on the same hook as the keys*. If you want to drink water before your coffee, put the glass of water *over the top of the coffee mug*. The "Stop-Doing" Prime

Environment design isn't just about making good habits easier; it's about making bad habits harder. This is Negative Priming.

- If the TV remote is on the coffee table, you will watch TV. If the remote is in a kitchen drawer and the batteries are in the laundry, you probably won't.

- If your phone is your alarm clock, you will scroll in bed. If your phone is in the kitchen and you bought a $10 analog alarm clock, you can't.

By designing your space to scream "DO THIS" for your stacks and "NOT THIS" for your distractions, you stop relying on your exhausted prefrontal cortex to make the right choice. You let the room make the choice for you.

The Stacking Assignment

It is time to stop theorizing and start building. To lock in the progress from the last eight chapters, you are going to pick one anchor and one attachment for the next 48 hours.

Do not pick three. Do not try to "overhaul your life." Pick one specific, tiny bridge and walk across it.

Step 1: Identify Your "Indestructible Anchor"

What is the one thing you do every single day without fail?

Making the first coffee/tea?

Putting your lunch plate in the sink?

Hanging up your car keys?

Sitting down in your office chair for the first time?

Step 2: Attach a "Two-Minute Win"

Pick a tool from the previous chapters and shrink it down until it's impossible to fail.

The Coffee Stack: Write your Three Things on a Post-it while the water boils.

The Chair Stack: Put your phone in the drawer the second your butt hits the seat.

The Sink Stack: Set a timer for a 5-Minute Rebellion as soon as the plate hits the water.

Step 3: Prime the Space

Tonight, before you go to bed, place the "tool" (the notebook, the timer, the "Phone Jail" box) directly on top of or next to the anchor. Make the cue unavoidable.

The "Don't Break the Chain" Tracker

For the next two days, your only goal is to protect this stack. If you do it, you win the day. It doesn't matter if the rest of the afternoon is a dumpster fire; if you hit your stack, you are rebuilding your neural pathways. You are proving to your brain that you are no longer a victim of your schedule—you are the architect of it.

The Transition: The Sunday-ish Liferaft

You've got the tactics. You've got the moves and tools. You've even got the automated habit stacks. Your days are starting to look like a coherent plan rather than a series of panicked reactions. But that was just this week… maintenance of course requires effort. You've have started to put these pieces in place, and maybe built the habits. However, if you break these habits what's to stop you from sliding back into that abyss again? Well, that's why it's also important to have a weekly reset.

Chapter 9: The Weekly Reset: Your Sunday(ish) Lifeline (Forgive Last Week, Pick Three Wins for This One)

Why "Resets" Beat "Resolutions"

Most productivity books tell you how to start a perfect streak. This book assumes your streak is going to break. It assumes you will get sick, your car will break down, or you'll simply spend three hours watching a documentary about competitive cheese-rolling when you were supposed to be doing a 5-Minute Rebellion.

The Weekly Reset is the "Reset Button" on an old Nintendo. It doesn't matter how badly you were losing the game; the moment you hit the button, the screen clears, the music restarts, and you are back at Level 1 with a full health bar.

The Sunday(ish) Concept: We call it "Sunday(ish)" because, while Sunday evening is a great time to map out the week, your brain doesn't care about the Gregorian calendar.

If your Tuesday is a disaster, your "Sunday(ish) Reset" happens on Wednesday morning. If you've been "offline" for a month, your Reset happens now.

The Reset is a 60-minute ritual where you stop doing and start mapping. It is the bridge between the chaos of what happened and the clarity of what's coming next. The following pillars are more like guidelines and suggestions – you pick which ones will you need the most – but if you don't know; then apply all and find your weak spot.

Pillar 1: The Forgiveness Protocol (The Emotional Audit)

Before you touch a calendar or a to-do list, you have to perform the most difficult task in this book: You have to forgive yourself for last week.

If you go into your planning session carrying the "debt" of everything you didn't finish last week, your new plan will be a suicide mission. You'll try to "make up for lost time" by scheduling a Heroic Monday (Chapter 8), which will lead to a Tuesday Face-Plant (Chapter 7), and the cycle will repeat.

The Forgiveness Audit:

Look at the "Undone": Look at the tasks you missed.

The Brutal Cut: If a task has been on your list for three weeks and hasn't killed you yet, it's probably not a "Three Thing." Delete it or move it back to the Analog Parking Lot.

The Clean Slate: Say it out loud: "Last week happened. It is data, not a character flaw. I am starting from zero."

You cannot build a "Robust" week on a foundation of guilt. The Reset starts by clearing the emotional cache so your brain has the "Decision Tokens" (Chapter 2) it needs to actually plan the next seven days.

Pillar 2: The Tactical Clear (Sorting the Confetti)

Once you've performed the Forgiveness Protocol, your brain is emotionally ready to plan. But your environment is likely still screaming for your attention. If you try to plan your week while sitting at a desk covered in random scraps of paper and 42 open browser tabs, your "Decision Fatigue" (Chapter 7) will kick in before you've even written a single word.

Pillar 2 is about The Tactical Clear. We are going to gather all the "confetti" of the last seven days and put it back into the system.

1. The Physical Sweep

Walk around your workspace. Pick up every receipt, every random sticky note, and every "I'll remember this later" scrap of paper. Don't process them yet. Just put them in one pile.

The Goal: Return your environment to its Primed State (Chapter 8).

The Rule: If it's trash, bin it. If it's a task, it goes into the Analog Parking Lot.

2. The Digital Defragmenter

Your computer is likely a visual representation of your internal chaos.

Close the Tabs: Be ruthless. If you haven't looked at that "Inspiration" tab in three days, bookmark it and kill it.

Clear the Desktop: Move those random screenshots and downloads into one folder labeled "To Sort" (or just delete them).

The Inbox Zero-ish: You don't need to answer every email. You just need to scan for "Landmines"—appointments or deadlines you missed that will blow up your next week.

   3.   Sorting the Analog Parking Lot

Now, look at that pile of notes and your Analog Parking Lot (Chapter 6). This is where the magic happens.

The Filter: Ask of every item: "Does this actually move the needle, or is it just 'Noise'?"

The Transfer: If it's a "Three Thing" for the coming week, circle it. If it's a "Someday" project, leave it in the lot. If it's a minor task, schedule a 5-Minute Rebellion to kill it.

By the end of the Tactical Clear, you should feel a physical sense of relief. The "background noise" of your life has been muted. You aren't reacting to the mess anymore; you are standing on top of it, looking out at the horizon.

Pillar 3: Calendar Combat (Mapping the Minefield)

Now that your desk is clear and your conscience is clean, it's time to look at the next seven days. Most people treat their calendar like a passive suggestion—a list of places they have to be. For the terminally disorganized, a calendar is a battle map.

If you don't look at the map before you start driving, you're going to hit a traffic jam on Tuesday, a road closure on Wednesday, and a multi-car pileup by Friday.

1.   Identifying the Landmines

Open your calendar and look for the "Red Zones."

Back-to-Backs: Where do you have meetings with zero "Buffer Time" (Chapter 4) between them?

The "Invisible" Deadlines: What tasks are due on Friday that you haven't started yet?

The Energy Drainers: Which appointments are going to leave you in a "Face-Plant" (Chapter 7) state?

2.   Placing the "Hard Rocks"

In the classic analogy, if you fill a jar with sand first, you can't fit the rocks. If you put the rocks in first, the sand fills the gaps.

Your Hard Rocks: These are your Three Wins for the week.

The Action: Physically block out 90-minute "Deep Work" sessions for these three items before the week starts. If they aren't on the calendar, they aren't real. They are just wishes.

3. Scheduling the "5-Minute Rebellions"

Look at the "Sand"—the small, annoying tasks like filing that one document or paying that bill.

The Move: Group them. Pick two "Admin Sprints" (30 minutes each) during the week where you will knock out as many tiny tasks as possible.

4. The "White Space" Defense

A perfect calendar is a trap. If every minute is booked, the first "Direct Sales" crisis or legal emergency will shatter your entire week.

The Rule: Leave at least 20% of your day as "White Space." This is your Contingency Buffer. It's the shock absorber for when life inevitably gets messy.

The Weekly Mantra: "I am not a victim of my schedule; I am the architect of my time. If I don't defend my 'Hard Rocks,' the 'Sand' will bury them."

By the end of Calendar Combat, you shouldn't just know where you have to be; you should know when you are going to win. You've identified the traps, you've built the bridges, and you've claimed your territory.

EXTRA: The Minimum Viable Reset (The 15-Minute Life-Raft)

There will be weeks where the "Sunday-ish Reset" feels like just another thing you're failing at. Maybe the kids are sick, a client emergency blew up your Sunday, or you're currently in the middle of a Wednesday "Face-Plant" and you only have the mental energy for a quick fix.

You don't need a 60-minute deep dive to stop the bleeding. You need the Minimum Viable Reset (MVR).

The 15-Minute "Emergency" Protocol:

The 3-Minute Brain Dump: Grab a piece of paper. Don't organize. Don't judge. Just scream every "to-do" currently rattling around your skull onto the page. Empty the cache.

The 5-Minute Calendar Scan: Open your calendar. Look at the next 48 hours only. Identify the one thing that will cause a disaster if you miss it.

The "Pick One" Win: Forget the "Three Things" for the week. Pick one thing you will do in the next 4 hours to feel like you've regained control. Just one.

The Physical Reset: Clear your immediate 2 feet of desk space. Throw away the trash. Close all your browser tabs except for the one you need for that "One Win."

The "I'm in the Car" Version

If you're literally commuting and can't write anything down, do a Vocal Reset. Use your phone's voice notes or just talk to the dashboard.

"Last week was a mess, and that's fine. I'm forgiving the undone tasks. Tomorrow, my only priority is X. I will deal with Y and Z in an Admin Sprint on Thursday."

Why the MVR Works

The MVR isn't about perfect planning; it's about Regulating Your Nervous System. When we are disorganized, our brain stays in "High-Alert" because it's trying to track a thousand invisible threads. The 15-minute reset makes those threads visible. Once they are visible, the "Chaotic Puppy" stops barking, and you can actually breathe.

Even a "bad" plan is better than no plan, because a plan gives you a place to return to when things get messy again.

The Reset Assignment

It is time to build your liferaft. If you wait until you "feel like" planning, you will only do it when things are already going well. We need this ritual to exist specifically for when things are going badly.

Step 1: The Calendar Stake

Open your calendar right now. Pick a 45-minute block.

The Traditionalist: Sunday at 7:00 p.m. (Pre-week clarity).

The Early Bird: Monday at 8:00 a.m. (The "Before the Storm" coffee).

The Realist: Friday at 4:00 p.m. (The "Close the Books" reset).

Step 2: The "Recurring" Rule

Set this as a weekly recurring appointment. Label it: "Sunday-ish Reset: The Liferaft." This is a non-negotiable meeting with the CEO of your life. You wouldn't blow off a high-stakes client; don't blow off the person who has to do the work.

Step 3: The "Draft One" Practice

Don't wait for your scheduled time. Do a 5-Minute MVR (Minimum Viable Reset) right now:

Forgive: One thing you "failed" at this week. Let it go.

Clear: Close every tab you aren't using for this book.

Pick: One "Three Thing" win for the next 24 hours.

The Golden Rule of the Reset:

You are not allowed to DO work during the Reset. You are only allowed to MAP the work. If you start answering emails, you've lost. Stay in the "Architect" role until the timer dings.

You've got the daily stacks. You've got the weekly reset. You finally have a map. But as you look at that map, you're going to notice something terrifying: The map is too full.

Even with the best "Three Things" list and a perfect Sunday Reset, you are still a human being with finite hours. For the terminally disorganized high-achiever, the biggest threat to your new system isn't "laziness"—it's Over-Commitment. It's the "Golden Cage" telling you that you can do it all if you just "work harder."

In the next chapter, we are going to learn the most powerful productivity tool in existence: life isn't always going to be perfect and fall in line with your plans, and that's okay!

Chapter 10: When It All Goes Pear-Shaped: Troubleshooting for Real Life (Because Murphy's Law Loves Productivity Plans)

The "Mike Tyson" Principle

The heavyweight boxer Mike Tyson once famously said, "Everyone has a plan until they get punched in the mouth." In the world of productivity, the "punch" rarely comes from a professional athlete. Usually, it's a 7:00 a.m. email from a client who has decided their minor inconvenience is now a Category 5 emergency. Or it's the overwhelming summer humidity suddenly deciding your laptop's cooling fan is optional. Or, most humbling of all, it's simply waking up and realizing that the "High-Performance CEO" version of yourself didn't get out of bed, and you've been replaced by a version of yourself that can't remember where they put their car keys.

We spend so much time building the "Perfect Tuesday" that when the "Punch" inevitably lands, we don't just lose the day—we lose our dignity. We feel like the system failed, or worse, that we are a fundamental failure.

But here is the secret the "gurus" don't tell you: The most productive people you know aren't the ones who never get punched. They are the ones who have learned how to go "limp" so the blow doesn't break their jaw. They've learned the art of the Strategic Pivot.

The Tale of the "Flaming Calendar"

I once knew a lawyer in my old city—let's call her Sarah—who lived by her color-coded Google Calendar. She had "Deep Work" blocks for her filings, "Buffer Zones" for her direct sales team, and even a "Mindfulness Minute" at 10:30 a.m. She was the poster child for Chapter 9's Weekly Reset.

One Wednesday, Sarah woke up ready to crush her "Three Things." By 9:15 a.m., her toddler had painted the hallway with organic beetroot juice, her lead paralegal had called in sick with the flu, and a major contract she'd been negotiating for six months had "hit a snag" that required an immediate, four-hour deep dive.

The old Sarah would have tried to "Power Through." She would have tried to do the contract and manage the team and scrub the beetroot juice, all while feeling a mounting sense of hysterical rage. She would have ended the day at 9:00 p.m. with a half-finished contract, a stained hallway, and a team that was terrified of her.

Instead, Sarah looked at her beautiful, color-coded calendar and metaphorically set it on fire.

She performed what I call the "Ceasefire." She sat in her car for three minutes, stared at the steering wheel, and admitted: "Today is not a 'Three Things' day. Today is a 'Survival' day." She deleted every non-essential meeting. She sent three short, blunt emails pushing deadlines to

Thursday. She accepted that she was going to be "Bad at her Job" for exactly six hours so she could be "Great at the Crisis" for four.

She didn't fail her plan. She pivoted to a new one.

The "Brain Fog" Wall: A Story of Zero Tokens

We've all had those days where the "Decision Tokens" (Chapter 2) aren't just low—they're non-existent.

I remember a marketing director who spent an entire Tuesday staring at a blank PowerPoint presentation. He had the coffee. He had the "Phone Jail" set up. He had the 5-Minute Rebellion timer ready to go. But every time he looked at the screen, his brain felt like it was made of damp cotton wool.

He spent four hours trying to work. He felt guilty, so he didn't take a break. He felt unproductive, so he didn't eat lunch. By 3:00 p.m., he was scrolling through Facebook marketplace looking at vintage lawnmowers he didn't need, drowning in shame.

The mistake wasn't the "Brain Fog." The mistake was the "Performance of Work." He was sitting in the chair, pretending to be a professional, while his "Hardware" was clearly offline for repairs.

If he had listened to the "Pear-Shaped" reality, he would have closed the laptop at noon, gone for a walk along the river, and accepted that Tuesday was a "Low-Octane" day.

He could have spent that time doing mindless admin—shredding paper, organizing his pens, or clearing his physical inbox—tasks that require zero Decision Tokens but still move the needle.

Instead, he fought the fog and let the fog win.

The "No-Guilt" Post-Mortem: A Tale of Two Mondays

There's a story I love about a high-level consultant who used to treat every "failed" day like a moral indictment. If he missed his morning workout or let a client call run into his "Deep Work" block, he didn't just adjust—he spiraled. He'd spend the evening replayng his "weakness" like a highlight reel of shame.

One Monday, his car battery died, his laptop decided to install a four-hour update, and he missed a crucial briefing. By noon, he was sitting on his kitchen floor eating cereal out of the box, convinced he was a fraud.

He called a mentor—a veteran lawyer who had survived thirty years of courtrooms and chaotic direct sales cycles. He expected a lecture on "grit."

Instead, the mentor laughed.

"You're treating your day like a court case where you're both the defendant and the hanging judge," the mentor said. "In my world, we call this 'Evidence.' Your car battery dying isn't a character flaw; it's a data point. Your laptop updating isn't a sign that you're lazy; it's an environmental constraint. Stop asking 'Why am I like this?' and start asking 'What happened to the system?'"

The consultant realized that he was wasting more energy on guilt than he was on the actual problem.

The "No-Guilt Post-Mortem" is the art of looking at a Day from Hell and treating it like a laboratory experiment. You look at the "Pear-Shaped" wreckage and ask:

Did the 'Chaotic Puppy' get out because I forgot to close the door (phone in another room)?

Did I hit the 'Brain Fog' wall because I tried to do a 'Hard Rock' task with zero 'Decision Tokens' left?

Or was it just a random act of a chaotic universe?

When you remove the shame, you gain the clarity to fix the leak. If the car battery died, you buy a jumper lead. If the laptop updated, you change your settings to "manual." But if you just sit there feeling guilty, you're essentially trying to jump-start a car with your own tears. It doesn't work, and it makes a mess of the upholstery.

Closing the Open Loops: The "I'm Human" Email

Finally, there's the story of the "Perfect Professional" who lived in fear of being found out. Whenever a day went pear-shaped and he missed a deadline, he would go 'Dark." He wouldn't answer his phone. He wouldn't reply to emails. He hoped that if he ignored the world long enough, the world would forget he existed.

Of course, the opposite happened. His silence created anxiety, and that anxiety turned into angry voicemails, which made him feel even more "Pear-Shaped."

One day, his sales team was waiting for a strategy doc that he simply hadn't finished because his brain had "Red-Lined." Instead of going Dark, he tried something terrifying: The Radical Truth.

He sent a one-sentence email: "Hey team, life has gone a bit pear-shaped today and I'm behind on the strategy doc. I'm taking the afternoon to reset and will have this to you by 10:00 a.m. tomorrow. Thanks for the grace."

The response? "No worries at all! Glad you're taking a breather. See you tomorrow."

The "Pear-Shaped" day didn't ruin his reputation. His honesty actually enhanced it. It turns out that everyone else is also struggling with their own "Chaotic Puppies" and "Brain Fog Walls." When you admit the day has gone sideways, you give everyone else permission to be human, too.

You close the "Open Loop" in your head, and suddenly, you can actually rest. You've stopped the "Big Slide" not through Herculean effort, but through the simple, quiet act of being real.

The beauty of a pear-shaped day is that it proves you are not a machine. A machine doesn't have "off" days; it just runs until it breaks. But you? You have rhythms. You have seasons. You have days where you are a legal shark and a marketing genius, and days where you are a human being who simply needs to stare at a tree for twenty minutes.

Accepting the "Pear-Shape" isn't about lowering your standards; it's about raising your self-awareness. When you stop fighting the reality of a bad day, you save the energy you need to make the next day a great one. You aren't "failing" the system—you're living the life the system was built to protect.

So, the next time the universe punches you in the mouth, don't worry about the plan. Just stay loose, breathe, and remember: Monday is a construct, but grace is a choice.

Chapter 11: You're Not Late – You're Right on Time (And Other Lies We Tell Ourselves… Until They're True)

Imagine for a moment that your life is a party you were supposed to host. You've spent the last few hours—or perhaps the last few decades—frantically cleaning the house, hiding the laundry that has achieved sentience, and agonizing over the fact that you still haven't figured out the "perfect" way to entertain. You feel behind. You feel like everyone else has already arrived, finished the appetizers, and moved on to the main course while you're still standing in the kitchen in mismatched socks.

But here is the final truth of this journey: the party doesn't actually start until you decide to walk into the room.

Throughout these pages, we've looked at the "Chaotic Puppy" that lives in your brain and realized that he isn't a flaw to be fixed, but a partner to be understood. We've stopped trying to be the person who wakes up at 4:00 AM for an ice bath and instead embraced the "No-Judgment Zone" of being a recovering chronic starter.

Think of how far you've come from that first "Tuesday afternoon rabbit hole". You've learned to stage a 5-Minute Rebellion when the mountain felt too high to climb. You've traded a suicide mission of forty-seven tasks for the sanity of the "Three Things" Rule. You've practiced

Distraction Jiu-Jitsu to turn your phone into a reluctant sidekick rather than an all-consuming enemy.

You've learned that rest isn't a moral failing, but a Strategic Recharge. You've built Habit Stacks that work with your brain instead of against it. And most importantly, you've discovered the power of the Weekly Reset—the liferaft that allows you to forgive last week and pick three new wins for this one.

Even when things went Pear-Shaped, you didn't let the "Big Slide" take you down. You realized that a "Half-Day Trap" doesn't mean the whole day is a write-off; it just means the second half is still up for grabs.

The "lie" we tell ourselves is that we are constantly late to our own potential. The truth is that you are exactly where you need to be to take the next step. You aren't aiming for a perfect, color-coded life; you're aiming to be slightly better than you were yesterday.

So, stop apologizing for the coffee mugs on your desk and the to-do lists that look like cries for help. You've finished the book. You've opened the door. You've officially joined the party.

The music is playing, the "Chaotic Puppy" is finally sitting still, and the afternoon is yours. You aren't late at all.

You're right on time.

THE "RIGHT ON TIME" CHEAT SHEET

A Survival Guide for the Terminally Disorganized

THE BRAIN HACKS (Mindset)

The Chaotic Puppy: Stop fighting your brain. It's not broken; it's just easily excited. Build fences (systems) instead of using a leash (willpower).

Decision Tokens: You only get a handful a day. Don't waste them on "What should I wear?" or "Which email first?" Save them for the big stuff.

The No-Judgment Zone: Shame is a productivity killer. If you've wasted half the day, forgive yourself immediately. You are right on time to start *now*.

THE DAILY TOOLKIT (Action)

The 5-Minute Rebellion: If a task feels like a mountain, commit to only 5 minutes. You can do anything for 300 seconds. Usually, starting is the only hard part.

The "Three Things" Rule: Your to-do list is not a wish list. Pick three non-negotiable wins. If you do those, the day is a victory. Everything else is a bonus.

The Analog Parking Lot: Your brain is for *having* ideas, not *holding* them. When a "Shiny Object" pops up, park it on paper and get back to your Three Things.

Distraction Jiu-Jitsu: Don't try to banish your phone; just make it harder to use. Move the apps, hide the charger, and let the "Puppy" find something else to chew on.

THE MOMENTUM BUILDERS (Systems)

Habit Stacking: Anchor new habits to things you already do. *"After I pour my coffee (Anchor), I will write my Three Things (New Habit)."*

The Sunday(ish) Reset: 45 minutes to clear the "confetti" of the past week. Forgive the undone, clear the desk, and map the "Hard Rocks" for the week ahead.

Strategic Recharging: Rest is a professional requirement. If you're hit by the "Afternoon Face-Plant," don't fake-work. Take a 20-minute reset so you can actually function later.

THE EMERGENCY PROTOCOL (Pear-Shaped Days)

The 60-Second Ceasefire: When it all goes wrong, stop moving. Breathe.

The Slash-and-Burn: Delete the non-essentials. If the day is a disaster, pick **one** Minimum Viable Win and let the rest go.

The Radical Truth: Don't go dark. Send the "I'm human" email. People respect honesty more than silence.

THE GOLDEN RULE:

Monday is a construct. Grace is a choice. You aren't failing the system; you're learning to drive a Ferrari in a world built for tractors. Now, pick one thing. Just one. Start now.

Epilogue – A Final Pep Talk (Or Whatever You Want To Call It)

(The Part Where You Actually Close the Book)

If you've made it this far, you've done something remarkable. For a person who identifies as "terminally disorganized," finishing a book about organization is equivalent to a cat successfully completing a course on underwater basket weaving. It's not just an achievement; it's a defiance of your own nature.

But as you stand here at the exit, I can see the look in your eyes. It's the "What If" look.

What if I wake up tomorrow and forget everything I just read? What if I lose my Three Things list by lunch? What if I'm just faking it and the Chaotic Puppy is actually the one in charge?

Here is my final pep talk: The version of you that started this book is not the version of you that is finishing it. You now possess the most dangerous weapon a disorganized person can have: Self-Awareness without the Shame. You know that your "Face-Plants" are biological, not moral. You know that your "Half-Day Traps" are just data points, not character flaws. You've stopped trying to be a person who never fails, and you've started being a person who knows exactly how to get back up.

You are a lawyer who understands the law of grace. You are a business owner who knows that the best investment you can make is in your own nervous system. You are a surgeon who isn't stressing about the blood on the floor, you're saving life (your own in this case). You are a high-achiever who has finally realized that the "Golden Cage" of perfectionism has no lock.

Don't wait for a "Fresh Start" on Monday. Don't wait for the stars to align or for your desk to be perfectly clear. The world is messy, your brain is wonderful, and the clock is ticking—but in the best possible way.

You have the tools. You have the permission. And for the first time in a long time, you aren't chasing the ghost of a "Perfect You" who doesn't exist. You are simply walking forward as the "Real You" who does.

Close this book. Put it on a shelf (or leave it on the floor, I won't judge). Take one deep breath.

Now, go be right on time for the rest of your life.

— *I.L. Hartley*

Recovering Chronic Starter

The End.

A Tiny Rebellion from You

Hey friend,

If this book helped even a little – if you laughed, felt seen, or stole even one tiny rebellion you're going to try – would you do me a huge favour?

Leave a quick, honest review on Amazon. It helps little authors myself continue to produce books like these (P.S I have another series in the pipeline).

No pressure, no guilt, and zero judgment if you don't. Either way, thank you for reading and for being exactly where you are right now.

You've got this.

— I.L. Hartley